Windows Server 2016 Security, Certificates, and Remote Access Cookbook

Recipe-based guide for security, networking and PKI in Windows Server 2016

Jordan Krause

BIRMINGHAM - MUMBAI

Windows Server 2016 Security, Certificates, and Remote Access Cookbook

Copyright © 2018 Packt Publishing

Commissioning Editor: Vijin Boricha
Acquisition Editor: Vinay Argekar
Content Development Editor: Aditi Gour
Technical Editor: Sushmeeta Jena
Copy Editor: Safis Editing
Project Coordinator: Hardik Bhinde
Proofreader: Safis Editing
Indexer: Aishwarya Gangawane
Graphics: Disha Haria
Production Coordinator: Deepika Naik

First published: April 2018

Production reference: 1250418

Published by Packt Publishing Ltd.
Livery Place
35 Livery Street
Birmingham
B3 2PB, UK.

ISBN 978-1-78913-767-5

www.packtpub.com

`mapt.io`

Mapt is an online digital library that gives you full access to over 5,000 books and videos, as well as industry leading tools to help you plan your personal development and advance your career. For more information, please visit our website.

Why subscribe?

- Spend less time learning and more time coding with practical eBooks and Videos from over 4,000 industry professionals

- Improve your learning with Skill Plans built especially for you

- Get a free eBook or video every month

- Mapt is fully searchable

- Copy and paste, print, and bookmark content

PacktPub.com

Did you know that Packt offers eBook versions of every book published, with PDF and ePub files available? You can upgrade to the eBook version at `www.PacktPub.com` and as a print book customer, you are entitled to a discount on the eBook copy. Get in touch with us at `service@packtpub.com` for more details.

At `www.PacktPub.com`, you can also read a collection of free technical articles, sign up for a range of free newsletters, and receive exclusive discounts and offers on Packt books and eBooks.

About the author

Jordan Krause is a six-time Microsoft MVP, currently awarded in the Cloud and Datacenter Management category. He has the unique opportunity to work daily with the Microsoft networking and remote access technologies as a Senior Engineer at IVO Networks. Jordan specializes in Microsoft DirectAccess and Always On VPN. Committed to continuous learning, Jordan holds certifications as an MCP, MCTS, MCSA, and MCITP Enterprise Administrator, and regularly writes articles reflecting his experiences with these technologies. Jordan lives and works in beautiful west Michigan (USA).

About the reviewer

Florian Klaffenbach is a solutions architect and consultant for Microsoft Infrastructure and cloud, specialized in Microsoft Hyper-V, Fileservices, System Center Virtual Machine Manager, and Microsoft Azure IaaS. He is also a cochairman of the Azure Community Germany. In April 2016, Microsoft awarded Florian the Microsoft Most Valued Professional for Cloud and Datacenter Management. Currently, he is working at MSG service AG as a senior consultant of Microsoft cloud infrastructure. He has also worked on many books by Packt Publishing.

Packt is searching for authors like you

If you're interested in becoming an author for Packt, please visit authors.packtpub.com and apply today. We have worked with thousands of developers and tech professionals, just like you, to help them share their insight with the global tech community. You can make a general application, apply for a specific hot topic that we are recruiting an author for, or submit your own idea.

Table of Contents

Preface

Microsoft is the clear leader of server racks in enterprise data centers across the globe. Walk into any backroom or data center of any company and you are almost guaranteed to find the infrastructure of that organization being supported by the Windows Server operating system. We have been relying on Windows Server for more than 20 years, and rightfully so—nowhere else can you find such an enormous mix of capabilities all provided inside one installer disc. Windows Server 2016 continues to provide the core functionality that we have
come to rely upon from all previous versions of Windows Server, but in better and more efficient ways. On top of that, we have some brand new capabilities in Server 2016 that are particularly mind-bending, new ways to accomplish more efficient and secure handling of our network traffic and data.

There is a relevant question mixed into all this server talk, "We hear so much about the cloud. Isn't everyone moving to the cloud? If so, why would we even need Windows Server 2016 in our company?" There are two different ways to answer this question, and both result in having huge benefits to knowing and understanding this newest version of Windows Server. First, there really aren't that many companies moving all of their equipment into the cloud. In fact, I have yet to meet any business with more than 10 employees who has gone all-in for the cloud. In almost all cases, it still makes sense that you would use at least one on premise server to manage local user account authentication, or DHCP, or print services, or for a local file server—the list goes on and on. Another reason companies aren't moving to the cloud like you might think they are is security. Sure, we might throw some data and some user accounts to the cloud to enable things like federation and ease of accessing that data, but what about sensitive or classified company data? You don't own your data if it resides in the cloud—you don't even have the capability to manage the backend servers that are actually storing that data alongside data from other companies. How can you be guaranteed of your data's security and survival? The ultimate answer is that you cannot, though there are steps being made in this direction. This alone keeps many folks that I have talked to away from moving some of their information to a cloud service provider.

The second reason it is still important to build knowledge on the Windows Server platform is that even if you have made the decision to move everything to the cloud, what server platform will you be running in the cloud that you now have to log into and administer? If you are using Azure for cloud services, there is a very good chance that you will be logging into Windows Server 2016 instances in order to administer your environment, even if those Server 2016 boxes are sitting in the cloud. So whether you have on premise servers, or you are managing servers sitting in the cloud somewhere, learning all you can about the new Windows Server 2016 operating system will be beneficial to your day job in IT.

When I first learned of the opportunity to put together this book, it was a difficult task to assemble an outline of possible recipes. Where to begin? There are so many different roles that can be run in Windows Server 2016, and so many tasks within each role that could be displayed. It was a natural reaction to start looking for all of the things that are brand new in Server 2016, and to want to talk only about recipes that display the latest and greatest features. But then I realized that those recipes on their own won't accomplish anything helpful for someone who is trying to learn about Windows Server administration for the first time. It is critical that we provide a base understanding of the important infrastructural roles that are commonly provided by Windows Server, because without that baseline the newest features won't amount to a hill of beans.

The recipes within this shortened volume are all accomplished using Windows Server 2016, but most companies still have a mix of 2016/2012R2/2012, and even 2008R2. Many of the recipes contained within can be beneficial to all of those server operating systems, helping you to strengthen security for all of your equipment and data. I hope that this book can also be a quick-reference guide that you keep near your desk into the future until you are fully versed and comfortable navigating around the new interface. Some recipes are clearly for the beginner, while others get deeper into the details so that someone already experienced with working inside Windows Server will gain some new knowledge out of reading this book. We will discuss some networking functions, and detail some security tasks that you can utilize to lock down your servers. Next covered is the very important topic of PKI and certificate distribution. Certificates are an extremely powerful tool for securing traffic and data on a network, it is vital that any server administrator understand how to utilize the Certification Authority role inside Windows Server. We will also walk through recipes regarding Microsoft's offerings in the Remote Access space, namely DirectAccess and VPN as you can use both of these roles to strengthen the security footprint of your enterprise.

A primary goal of this cookbook is to be a reference guide that you can come back to time and again when you need to accomplish common tasks in your environment, but want to ensure that you are performing them the right way. I hope that through these chapters you are able to become comfortable enough with Windows Server 2016 that you will go out and install it today!

Who this book is for

This book is for system administrators and IT professionals that may or may not have previous experience with Windows Server 2012 R2 or its predecessors. Since the start of this book, I have been contacted and asked many times whether the core, baseline information to beginning to work with Windows Server will be included. These requests have come from current desktop administrators wanting to get into the server world, and even from developers hoping to better understand the infrastructure upon which their applications run. Both will benefit from the information provided here. Anyone hoping to acquire the skills and knowledge necessary to manage and maintain the core infrastructure required for a Windows Server 2016 environment should find something interesting on the pages contained within.

What this book covers

Chapter 1, *Security and Networking*, teaches us some methods for locking down access on our servers. We will also cover commands which can be very useful tools as you start monitoring network traffic.

Chapter 2, *Working with Certificates*, will start to get us comfortable with the creation and distribution of certificates within our network. PKI is an area that is becoming more and more prevalent, but the majority of server administrators have not yet had an opportunity to work hands-on with them.

Chapter 3, *Remote Access*, digs into using your Server 2016 as the connectivity platform which brings your remote computers into the corporate network. We discuss DirectAccess and VPN in this chapter.

To get the most out of this book

All the technologies and features that are discussed in the recipes of this book are included with Windows Server 2016. As long as you have access to the operating system installer disc and either a piece of hardware or a virtualization environment where you can spin up a new virtual machine, you will be able to install the operating system and follow along with our lessons.

Many of the tasks that we are going to accomplish together require a certain amount of base networking and infrastructure to be configured, in order to fully test the technologies that we are working with. The easiest method to working through all of these recipes will be to have access to a Hyper-V server upon which you can build multiple virtual machines that run Windows Server 2016. With this available, you will be able to build recipe upon recipe as we move through setting up the core infrastructural tasks, and then utilize those same servers to build upon in the later recipes. Building a baseline lab network running Server 2016 for the Microsoft infrastructure roles like Active Directory, DNS, and DHCP will help you tremendously as you move throughout this book and your job in IT.

Download the color images

We also provide a PDF file that has color images of the screenshots/diagrams used in this book. You can download it here: `http://www.packtpub.com/sites/default/files/downloads/WindowsServer2016SecurityCertificatesandRemoteAccessCookbook_ColorImages.pdf`.

Conventions used

There are a number of text conventions used throughout this book.

`CodeInText`: Indicates code words in text, database table names, folder names, filenames, file extensions, pathnames, dummy URLs, user input, and Twitter handles. Here is an example: "Mount the downloaded `WebStorm-10*.dmg` disk image file as another disk in your system."

A block of code is set as follows:

```
html, body, #map {
  height: 100%;
  margin: 0;
  padding: 0
}
```

When we wish to draw your attention to a particular part of a code block, the relevant lines or items are set in bold:

```
[default]
exten => s,1,Dial(Zap/1|30)
exten => s,2,Voicemail(u100)
exten => s,102,Voicemail(b100)
exten => i,1,Voicemail(s0)
```

Any command-line input or output is written as follows:

```
$ mkdir css
$ cd css
```

Bold: Indicates a new term, an important word, or words that you see onscreen. For example, words in menus or dialog boxes appear in the text like this. Here is an example: "Select **System info** from the **Administration** panel."

Warnings or important notes appear like this.

Tips and tricks appear like this.

Get in touch

Feedback from our readers is always welcome.

General feedback: Email feedback@packtpub.com and mention the book title in the subject of your message. If you have questions about any aspect of this book, please email us at questions@packtpub.com.

Errata: Although we have taken every care to ensure the accuracy of our content, mistakes do happen. If you have found a mistake in this book, we would be grateful if you would report this to us. Please visit www.packtpub.com/submit-errata, selecting your book, clicking on the Errata Submission Form link, and entering the details.

Piracy: If you come across any illegal copies of our works in any form on the Internet, we would be grateful if you would provide us with the location address or website name. Please contact us at copyright@packtpub.com with a link to the material.

If you are interested in becoming an author: If there is a topic that you have expertise in and you are interested in either writing or contributing to a book, please visit authors.packtpub.com.

Reviews

Please leave a review. Once you have read and used this book, why not leave a review on the site that you purchased it from? Potential readers can then see and use your unbiased opinion to make purchase decisions, we at Packt can understand what you think about our products, and our authors can see your feedback on their book. Thank you!

For more information about Packt, please visit `packtpub.com`.

Security and Networking 1

Various breaches and vulnerabilities over the past few years have brought security to the forefront of all IT Administrators' minds. In a Windows Server 2016 environment, there are many functions you can enable to lock down security on your own network. Let's explore some of these functions, as well as practice with some tools and tricks that can help us to better understand and navigate our own networks. We will also take a look at some common networking tasks that will help you out in your day-to-day work. In this chapter, we will look at the following recipes:

- Requiring complex passwords in your network
- Using Windows Firewall with Advanced Security to block unnecessary traffic
- Changing the RDP port on your server to hide access
- Multi-homing your Windows Server 2016
- Adding a static route into the Windows routing table
- Using Telnet to test a connection and network flow
- Using the Pathping command to trace network traffic
- Setting up NIC Teaming
- Renaming and domain joining via PowerShell
- Building your first Server Core

Introduction

In this chapter, we are going to tackle a number of tasks related to networking your Windows Server 2016 machines and locking down that environment a little bit by enabling some security functions. Some of the tools we are going to use can be very useful for daily tasks, and I hope that the steps we take will prompt you to start some gears spinning in your own mind to investigate deeper into taking full advantage of what Microsoft has to offer within this operating system.

Requiring complex passwords in your network

With the tools that attackers have available today, simple passwords should be outlawed by every company. Turning on the requirement for complex passwords in your network is pretty simple; the hard part is knowing where to find the setting. We are going to require complex passwords by making a change inside Group Policy. We will be using Group Policy in a step-by-step fashion, and combining this recipe with the chapter on Group Policy in the book *Windows Server 2016 Administration Cookbook,* published by Packt, will give you even more creativity in the way that you could later change the implementation of this password policy.

Getting ready

We need to be working in a domain environment, as Group Policy is something that runs within Active Directory. The change that we are going to make in Group Policy is done from a domain controller, and we will utilize a client computer to test our policy once it has been implemented.

How to do it...

The following steps will help you enable complex passwords for your network:

1. On your domain controller, launch **Group Policy Management** from inside the **Tools** menu in **Server Manager**.

2. Expand your forest name and find the name of your domain inside the `Domains` folder. If you expand your domain name, you will see a **Group Policy Object (GPO)** in there called the **Default Domain Policy**. This policy is automatically configured in a new Active Directory environment to apply to all user accounts, so for this recipe, we will modify this GPO to require complex passwords for all of our users.

3. Right-click on **Default Domain Policy** and click **Edit...**:

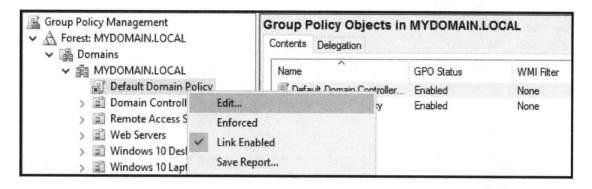

You can easily create a new GPO and use it instead of modifying the built-in default policy. This will give you better control over who or what gets the settings applied to them. See the chapter *Group Policy* from the book, *Windows Server 2016 Administration Cookbook,* for more detail on managing the GPOs themselves. We use the **Default Domain Policy** in this recipe for the sake of shortening the number of steps you need to take, but it really is recommended never to use the **Default Domain Policy** to make actual changes in a production environment.

4. Browse to the following location by navigating to **Computer Configuration** | **Policies** | **Windows Settings** | **Security Settings** | **Account Policies** | **Password Policy**.

5. Here are the configurable options that you can set for password requirements in your network. I am going to set **Maximum password age** to 30 days so that everyone needs to change their password monthly, and I will increase **Minimum password length** to 8 characters. I will also enable the complexity requirements setting, which sets a number of different requirements. If you double-click on that setting and browse to the **Explain** tab, you will see a list of all the items that are now required:

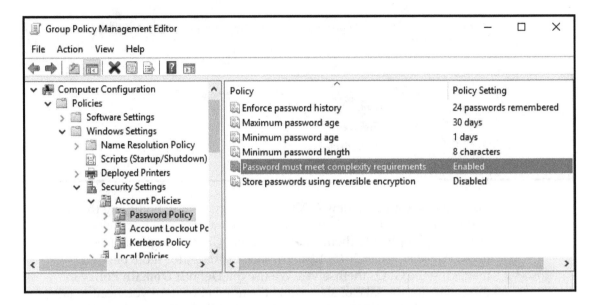

6. Now go ahead and try logging into a computer with a domain user account and come to discover that our password no longer meets the criteria and we have to change it accordingly:

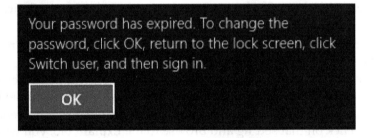

How it works...

Because we set requirements for password complexity in the Default Domain Policy, that requirement flows across our whole network. A solid password policy is very important in today's networks and just scratches the surface of Group Policy's abilities. These simple setting changes can make the difference in whether or not your company is compromised as a result of a brute force password attack.

Using Windows Firewall with Advanced Security to block unnecessary traffic

I encounter far too many networks with policies in place that disable the built-in **Windows Firewall with Advanced Security** (**WFAS**) by default on all of their machines. Usually, if I ask about this, the reason is either unknown or *It's always been that way*. I think this is a carry-over from the Windows XP/Server 2003 days, or maybe even older, when the Windows Firewall was less than desirable. Believe me when I tell you that WFAS in today's operating systems is very advanced, stable, and beneficial. If you want to stop unnecessary or malicious traffic from getting to your server, look no further than this built-in tool.

Getting ready

We are going to use two Windows Server 2016 machines for this task. We will test connectivity between the two to set our baseline and then create a rule that blocks the functions we just tested. Next, we will test again to ensure that our changes did what we expected them to, blocking the traffic that we attempt to generate. It is important to set up a baseline of tests and run those same tests following each change to ensure the rules are working exactly as you want them to.

How to do it...

If you want to stop unnecessary traffic from getting to your server, execute the following instructions:

1. First, we want to test the existing connectivity. I log into my DC2 server, and from there I am able to successfully execute the `ping web1` command and get a reply. I can also open up File Explorer and browse to \\WEB1 and see a folder shared there. This baseline test tells me that both ICMP (ping) traffic and file access are currently open and allowed by WFAS on WEB1. We want to stop these functions from happening.
2. Log in to WEB1 and open **Windows Firewall with Advanced Security**. You can open this either from the Start screen and typing it in, or by opening a **Run** prompt and typing `wf.msc`.

3. Inside WFAS, your two best friends when trying to control traffic are the **Inbound Rules** and **Outbound Rules** sections on the left. You need to think of Inbound and Outbound from the server's perspective. Inbound Rules manipulate traffic that is flowing in toward your server, and Outbound Rules handle traffic flowing out of your server toward the rest of the network. If you click on **Inbound Rules**, you will see the list of preconfigured rules that exist already.

4. Right-click on **Inbound Rules** and click on **New Rule...**.

5. First, let's make a rule to block the file access from happening. Choose **Port** and on the next screen, enter the value for port **TCP** as `445`. Then you realize that you might as well also block RDP access since that is also currently enabled. No problem! Simply comma separate these numbers as follows:

Does this rule apply to all local ports or specific local ports?

○ **All local ports**

◉ **Specific local ports:**   445, 3389|

Example: 80, 443, 5000-5010

---

6. Choose **Block the connection**.

7. On the next screen where you choose which firewall profile the rule applies to, you can leave it set to all three checked as the default. This will ensure that the rule will apply to any NIC that has any firewall profile assigned. If you only have a single NIC on your server and it is joined to the domain, then you could get away with only selecting the domain profile if you wanted to deselect the other two. For our recipe, I'm going to leave them all checked.

8. Type any kind of descriptive name for your rule—something like `Block File and RDP Access`.

9. You did it! You will see that the new rule exists, and it is immediately put into action. If you head over to your other server, you will now find that you can no longer RDP or browse the file shares at all on WEB1.

10. We can still successfully ping WEB1, though, and we wanted to put a stop to that as well. To stop ICMP traffic, you simply need to create another rule. This one is a little bit more complicated, though. First, go ahead and create a second Inbound Rule, and use the exact same settings that you used for your RDP file rule. You can enter anything into the **Port** field; it doesn't matter because we will be invalidating it in a minute, so maybe use port 445 for our example.

11. Great, now you have two rules in there that are both blocking port 445. That doesn't do us much good. Right-click on the newest rule that we just created, head into **Properties**, and let's improve this rule a little bit.

12. Inside the **Protocols and Ports** tab, drop down the **Protocol** type and choose ICMPv4. That's all you have to do! You have now modified this rule so that it is no longer blocking TCP port 445, but rather this rule is now blocking ICMPv4 traffic:

13. If you log back into DC2, we no longer receive ping replies when trying to contact the WEB1 server.

Take some time to play around inside the **Scope** tab. This section of a WFAS rule allows you to scope the rule down so that it only applies to particular IP addresses or ranges. Maybe you only want to block file share access from a particular subnet or only for the external NIC of an edge server. Requirements like these are easy to accomplish!

How it works...

We used the Windows Firewall with Advanced Security to create a couple of simple rules to block unwanted traffic coming into our server. These rules are put into place immediately and are very easy to generate. What is even greater is that our WFAS rules can be created centrally by making use of Group Policy so that you don't even have to touch the individual servers to apply connection rules to them. WFAS is very different than the Windows Firewall of 10 years ago, and if you are not making use of it today I seriously recommend that you reconsider.

Changing the RDP port on your server to hide access

Everybody uses RDP. Attackers and bots, curiously, also know that *everybody* uses RDP. If you are working with perimeter servers that are potentially connected to the Internet, having RDP enabled can be especially dangerous because it is quite easy to leave your server in a state where it is open from outside of your network. This gives anyone the ability to start guessing passwords or trying to brute force their way into your server, or just a way to give you some denial-of-service headaches by throwing thousands of login attempts at that server.

Even aside from the worries of potential access from the public Internet, you may want to ensure that regular users aren't trying to poke around where they shouldn't be by opening up RDP connections to servers within your network. There are a few ways that you could restrict this access. You could come up with some creative firewall rules that only allow RDP access from certain subnets, and try to contain your IT computers to those subnets. Or maybe you could configure RDP on your destination servers to require certificates as part of the authentication process, thus only allowing users with those certificates to have access. These are both fairly complicated. I like to employ a much simpler solution to keep unwanted eyes from seeing my RDP login screens.

Change the port that RDP runs on! What? Can you do that? Yes, RDP by default listens and connects on TCP port 3389. The Remote Desktop client that is installed on almost every client machine everywhere automatically assumes that the server they are connecting to is listening on 3389, and so you don't even have to specify a port when you try to connect. There isn't even a field for it in the client. So it's pretty rare that I talk to people (even IT people) who know that 3389 is the default. Given that, if we were able to change that 3389 to something different, something of our own choosing, I think that would do a grand job of keeping people out of our systems. Let's say we have a sensitive server and want to keep access to a minimum. Let's change the RDP port on that to something only we know, maybe port 4822. That'll keep 'em guessing for a while.

Getting ready

Any Windows Server 2016 machine will do for this task. We are going to set our custom RDP port on WEB1, and then we are going to test accessing it from a Windows 10 client machine.

How to do it...

Go through the following steps to change the RDP port to one of your liking:

1. Open **Registry Editor**. You can do this by going to either the **Start** screen or Command Prompt and typing regedit.

2. Browse to:
   HKEY_LOCAL_MACHINE\SYSTEM\CurrentControlSet\Control\Terminal
   Server\WinStations\RDP-Tcp.

3. Find the value called **PortNumber** and change it to 4822:

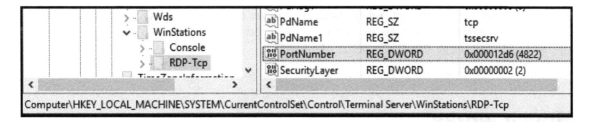

4. Restart the server.

5. Now log into your client computer and open up **Remote Desktop Connection** by typing that name into your **Start** screen. You can also type mstsc in Command Prompt to open this program. If you try to connect directly to WEB1, your connection will fail as the server is no longer listening on the standard port 3389.

Enter in `WEB1:4822` and you connect successfully:

If at first you cannot connect, make sure to check your Windows Firewall settings. It is possible that you may need to add a rule to WFAS on the server to allow port 4822.

How it works...

With a simple registry change, we can adjust the RDP listener port on servers. This will help keep unwanted RDP connections from being made, which can be useful both inside and outside the corporate network. After making this change, the only people who will be able to reach the RDP login screen would be those who know your new RDP port, and who know how to utilize that custom port within the remote desktop connection tool.

Multi-homing your Windows Server 2016

Historically, there haven't been many scenarios that require Windows servers to have more than a single network card. This is because most of the roles that they were accomplishing were done on whatever single network they were plugged into. There was no need for a server to have direct connections to multiple networks because that was the router and switch's job, right? In today's Windows Server world, there are numerous roles that can take advantage of multi-homing, which simply means having multiple NICs connected to different networks at the same time. There are some proxy roles that can use multiple NICs; Remote Access roles such as DirectAccess and VPN recommend a dual-NIC setup, and you can even use a Windows Server as a general router if you want to.

I work a lot with DirectAccess and I find many multi-homed servers with incorrect network configurations. This recipe is a collection of points that need to be followed when configuring a Windows Server with multiple NICs to make sure it behaves and flows traffic as you expect it to.

Getting ready

You just need a Windows Server 2016 online for this one. We have two NICs installed on this server and they are plugged into different networks. I am prepping a Remote Access server that will sit on the edge, so I have one NIC plugged into the corporate internal network, while the other NIC is connected to the Internet.

How to do it...

To configure a Windows Server with multiple NICs, perform the following process:

- **Only one Default Gateway**: In your NIC properties, you need to make sure that you only have a Default Gateway identified on *one* of your NICs. This is the most common mistake that I find in the field. If you have two NICs, it would seem logical that you would simply populate their IP address settings just like you would with any server or computer, right? Nope. The purpose of a Default Gateway is to be the fallback or the route of last resort. Whenever your server tries to send out network traffic, it will search the local routing table for information on how to send out that traffic. If it does not find a specific route that corresponds to the IP address that you are sending to, then it will default that traffic over to the Default Gateway address. Therefore, you only ever want to have one Default Gateway assigned on a server, no matter how many NICs are connected. On all other NICs installed on the system, simply leave the Default Gateway field unpopulated inside the TCP/IP properties. By the way, for a DirectAccess server or for pretty much any other server that faces the Internet, the Default Gateway needs to be on the External NIC, so I will be leaving that field empty in the properties of my Internal NIC.

- **Limit your DNS servers**: Another common configuration that I have seen is to have DNS server addresses defined for every network adapter installed on the system. While this doesn't usually break anything like multiple Default Gateways can, it does cause unnecessary slowness when the system is trying to resolve DNS names. Try to have DNS server addresses configured on only one NIC. Once again, using our example DirectAccess server setup, I will be configuring DNS server addresses on my Internal NIC because that is necessary for DA to work. I will not be putting my public DNS server specifications into the External NIC; instead, I will leave those fields empty.

- **Use static IP addresses**: The roles and functions you may perform on a Windows Server that requires multiple NICs will be best served by having static IP address information assigned to those network cards. If you let one or more of the NICs pull information from DHCP, you could easily create a situation where you have too many DNS servers defined, or where you have multiple Default Gateways on your system. As we already know, neither of these scenarios is desirable.

- **Prioritize the NIC binding**: It is a good practice to set a priority for your NICs so you can place the card that you expect to have the most network traffic as #1 in the list. For our DirectAccess server, we always want the Internal NIC to be placed on the top, so let's make sure that is set correctly using the following steps:

    1. Open up **Network and Sharing Center** and click on **Change adapter settings** so that you are in the **Network Connections** screen where you can see the network cards installed on your system.
    2. Now press the *Alt* key on your keyboard and you will see the menus at the top of this window.
    3. Head into the **Advanced** menu and click on **Advanced Settings....** Now simply make sure that your **Internal** NIC is listed on top:

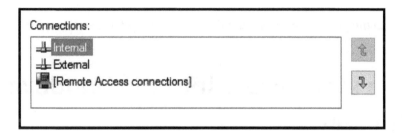

 The NIC binding prioritization order is a function that is no longer necessary in Windows Server 2016. The instructions are still included here because they apply to any older Windows Server operating systems, and should be followed on those platforms.

- **Add static routes**: A couple of minutes ago, you probably started thinking "Hey, if I don't have a Default Gateway on my Internal NIC, what tells the server how to get packets into the subnets of my internal network?" Great question! Because you only have one Default Gateway, when you need to send traffic out one of the other NICs, you need to make sure that a static route exists in the Windows routing table. This ensures that the server knows which interface gets traffic for each subnet. Make sure to check out our next recipe for specific information on how to add those routes.

How it works...

Anybody can multi-home their server by simply plugging two NICs into two different networks. The tricky part is making sure that you configure those NICs and the operating system appropriately so that network traffic flows in the right directions at the right times. Following this list of rules will give you a solid foundation so that you can build out these types of scenarios and know that you are doing so in the correct fashion. Deviating from these rules will result in unexpected behavior, which sometimes is not immediately obvious. This can make for some very frustrating troubleshooting down the road.

See also

- The *Adding a static route into the Windows routing table* recipe

Adding a static route into the Windows routing table

This recipe follows right on the heels of our previous topic. If you have never worked on a server that is making use of more than one NIC, then you have probably never had a reason to poke around in the Windows routing table. The minute that you are tasked with setting up a new server that needs to be connected to multiple networks, or that you get thrown into a situation where you need to troubleshoot such a system, this suddenly becomes critical information to have in your back pocket.

On a server that is connected to multiple networks, you only have one Default Gateway address defined. This means any subnets that need to be reached by flowing through one of the other NICs, the ones that do not contain the Default Gateway, need to be specifically defined inside the routing table. Otherwise, Windows simply does not know how to get to those subnets and it will attempt to push all traffic through the Default Gateway. This traffic will never make it to its destination and communications will fail.

Today, we are setting up a new VPN server. This server has a NIC plugged into the Internet where remote clients will come in, and another NIC plugged into the internal network so that the client traffic can make its way to the application servers that the users need to access. In this scenario, the Default Gateway must be populated on the External NIC. There will be no Default Gateway address defined on the Internal NIC, and without some assistance, Windows will have no idea how to properly route traffic toward the servers inside the network.

For our example, the Internal NIC is plugged into the 10.0.0.x network. Since it has a direct physical connection to this network, it is automatically able to properly contact other servers that reside on this subnet. So if the VPN server was 10.0.0.5 and we had a domain controller running on 10.0.0.2, we would be able to contact that domain controller without any additional configuration. But most companies have multiple subnets inside their network. So what if our VPN users needed to contact a web server that is sitting on the 10.0.1.x network? When traffic comes into the VPN server looking for a destination of 10.0.1.8 (the web server), the VPN server will check its local routing table and find that it does not have an entry for the 10.0.1.x network. Since it doesn't know what to do with this request, it sends it to the Default Gateway, which sends the packets back out the External NIC. Those packets don't have a valid destination to reach through the External NIC, which is plugged into the Internet, and so the traffic simply fails.

We need to define a static route in the routing table of our VPN server, so that when VPN clients request resources inside the 10.0.1.x network, then that traffic makes its way to the destination network successfully. We need to bind this route to our Internal NIC so that the VPN server knows it has to send these packets through that physical network interface.

Getting ready

We are setting up a new Windows Server 2016 VPN server. This server has two NICs installed, one plugged into the Internet and the other plugged into the internal network. Inside our corporate network, there are two subnets. 10.0.0.x (/24), which our Internal NIC is plugged into, and 10.0.1.x (/24), where our web server resides. There is, of course, a router between the two internal subnets, which is how traffic physically flows between the two. The IP address of that router is 10.0.0.254. If we were able to configure a Default Gateway on the Internal NIC of our VPN server, it would be set to 10.0.0.254, and all traffic would work without any further input. However, since our VPN server is multi-homed and there can only be a Default Gateway configured on the External NIC, we need to tell the server that it has to push 10.0.1.x traffic through 10.0.0.254 by using the Internal NIC.

How to do it...

So basically, we need to do the following to create a static route in our VPN server:

- Identify the subnet that we want to contact. In our example, it is `10.0.1.0`
- Identify the subnet mask, which is `255.255.255.0`
- Identify the IP address of the router that will get us to that network, which is `10.0.0.254`
- Identify the Interface ID number of the physical NIC that needs to carry this traffic, which can be attained as follows:
    1. Discovering this NIC ID is going to take us a minute. First, open up **Network Connections** and expand the fields so that you can see the device name of each NIC:

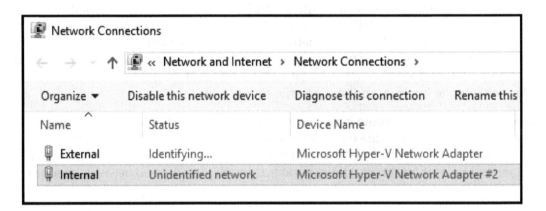

2. Now open Command Prompt and type `route print`. This is a print of your entire routing table. Scroll back up to the very top and you will see the Interface ID numbers of your NICs listed:

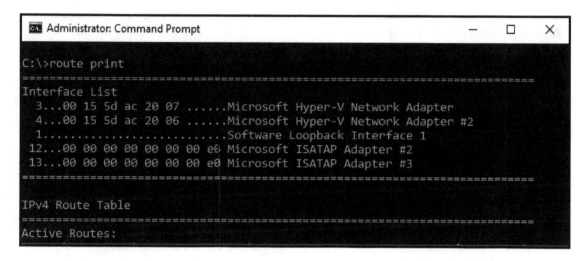

We can see that our Internal NIC is the second NIC, named `Microsoft Hyper-V Network Adapter #2`. Looking at that entry in the route print, there is a number over to the left of that name. This is our Internal NIC's Interface ID number, which is `4` in this example.

We now have all the information needed to put together our route statement and bind it to our Internal NIC. The general format that our route add statement needs to take is `route add -p <subnet> mask <mask> <gateway> if <interfaceID>`. The `-p` part of the command is very important as it makes this route persistent. Without the `-p` part, our new route would disappear after the reboot.

So, in order to tell our VPN server how to send traffic into the new 10.0.1.x subnet that we have been talking about, our specific command is as follows:

```
route add -p 10.0.1.0 mask 255.255.255.0 10.0.0.254 if 4
```

This command tells the server to add a new persistent route for the 10.0.1.0/24 network, flow this network traffic through the `10.0.0.254` gateway and bind this route to NIC ID 4, which is our internal network interface.

How it works...

With a multi-homed server, only one NIC will have a Default Gateway. Therefore, any subnets that we need to access through the other interfaces have to be specifically defined. Before we added this new route, the server was completely unable to contact the 10.0.1.x network. This is because the routing table did not have any information about this subnet, so any traffic trying to get there was being sent out the Default Gateway, which is on the External NIC plugged into the Internet. By adding a static route to our server, we have now defined a routing path for the server to take whenever it has traffic that needs to get to 10.0.1.x.

If you have many subnets in your network, you may be able to cover them all with a blanket route statement. A *blanket route* is also known as an aggregate or supernet route. This could save you the time of having to set up a new route statement for each and every one of your networks. For example, if we had many *10.something* networks and we wanted to flow all of them through our Internal NIC, we could do that with a single route statement, as follows:

```
Route add -p 10.0.0.0 mask 255.0.0.0 10.0.0.254 if 4
```

This route would send any 10.x.x.x traffic through the Internal NIC. Whether you blanket your routes like this or set each one up individually doesn't make a difference to the server as long as its routing table contains information about where to send the packets that it needs to process.

Using Telnet to test a connection and network flow

The `ping` command has always been an IT person's best friend to do quick network connection checks. How many of you are the family and neighborhood go-to guy to fix anything with buttons? I'm guessing most of you. And as such, if someone told you they were having trouble accessing the Internet from their laptop at home, what is the first thing you would do when you showed up? Try to ping their router, a website, or another computer in their network. You know you would! This has always been a wonderfully quick and easy way to test whether or not you have network traffic flowing between two endpoints. The same troubleshooting procedure exists in all workplaces and corporations. I have even seen many monitoring tools and scripts utilize the results of whether or not a ping replies to report on whether or not a particular service is up and running. If you get a ping reply, it's working, and if it times out, it's down, right?

Not necessarily. The problem we are here to address today is that more and more networks and routers are starting to block ICMP traffic by default. Pings = ICMP. This means that you can no longer take your ping test results to the bank. If your network connection traverses a router or firewall that blocks ICMP, your ping test will time out, even if the service is up and running. Windows Firewall even blocks ICMP by default now. So if you bring a new server online in your network and give it an IP address, you may notice that attempting to ping that new server results in timeouts. There is nothing wrong with the server, and it is capable of sending and receiving network traffic, but the local firewall on that server is blocking the incoming ping request.

I only lay out this information to let you know that `ping` is no longer the best tool for determining a connection between machines. Today's recipe will introduce a tool that has been around for a long time, but that I don't find many administrators taking advantage of. This is the Telnet Client, which I use on a daily basis. I hope that you will too!

Getting ready

We have a Server 2016 web server that has a website running. It is also enabled for RDP access and file sharing, but ICMP is being blocked by the local Windows Firewall. We are going to run some tests with a client machine against this server to try to determine which services are up and running.

How to do it...

To start working with Telnet Client, have a look at these instructions:

1. First, just to prove our point here, let's open up Command Prompt on our testing client machine and try to ping WEB1 using the `ping web1` command. Because ICMP is being blocked by the firewall, all we get is a series of timeouts:

```
Administrator: Command Prompt                             —    □    ×

Pinging web1.MYDOMAIN.LOCAL [10.0.0.85] with 32 bytes of data:
Request timed out.
Request timed out.
Request timed out.
Request timed out.

Ping statistics for 10.0.0.85:
    Packets: Sent = 4, Received = 0, Lost = 4 (100% loss),

C:\>
```

2. Now let's use the `Telnet` command to accomplish some more intuitive digging into whether or not WEB1 is online and functional. Note that Telnet Client is not available inside Command Prompt by default; it is a Windows feature that must be installed. On the client machine we are using to test, head into **Control Panel** | **Programs** | **Turn Windows features on or off** (or **Server Manager** if your testing machine is a server) and choose to add roles or features. We want to install the feature called Telnet Client. Alternatively, you can install the Telnet Client feature with a simple PowerShell command:

```
Install-WindowsFeature Telnet-Client
```

3. Now we have the `telnet` command available to use inside Command Prompt. The general format of the command goes like this: `telnet <server> <port>`. When you run this command, you are effectively saying "Let's try to create a connection to this server name, on this particular port."

4. Even though we cannot ping WEB1, let's try to use `telnet` to open a connection to port 80, which is the website that we have running. The command is as follows:

telnet web1 80

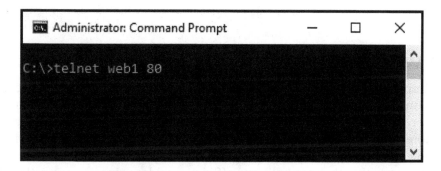

5. When we press *Enter*, the Command Prompt window changes to a flashing cursor. This is your confirmation that Telnet was able to open a successful connection to port 80 on the WEB1 server:

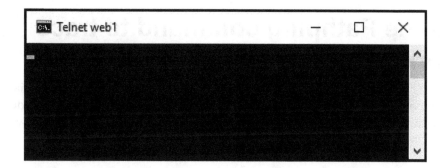

6. Now try using the `telnet 10.0.0.85 3389` command. This also results in a flashing cursor, indicating that we successfully connected to port 3389 (RDP) on IP address 10.0.0.85. This is the IP address of WEB1. I wanted to show this to point out that you can use either names or IP addresses with your `telnet` commands.

7. And finally, how about `telnet web1 53`? This one results in a timeout, and we do not see our flashing cursor. So it appears that port 53 is not responding on the WEB1 server, which makes sense because port 53 is commonly used by DNS, and this is a web server, not a DNS server. If we were to query one of our domain controllers that is also running DNS, we would be able to make a successful telnet connection to port 53 on those guys.

Telnet queries work with TCP traffic, which covers most services that you will be polling for. Telnet does not have a connector for UDP ports.

How it works...

Telnet is a simple but powerful command that can be run to query against particular ports and services on your servers. When trying to determine whether or not a particular service is available, or when trying to troubleshoot some form of network connectivity problem, it is a much more reliable tool than using a simple `ping` request. If you have been thinking about building some kind of script that programmatically reaches out and checks against servers to report whether they are online or offline, consider using `telnet` rather than `ping` so that you can query the individual service that the system is providing by using its particular port number.

Using the Pathping command to trace network traffic

When building or troubleshooting a network connection, it is often very beneficial to be able to watch the path that your packets take as they make their way from source to destination. Or perhaps they never make it to the destination and you want to figure out how far they do travel before stopping so that you can focus your work efforts in that area.

One command that has been used by network admins for years is traceroute (`tracert`), but the output contains some information that is often unnecessary, and the output is missing one large key ingredient. Namely, traceroute shows the first hop as the first router that you traverse and does not show you what physical NIC the packets are flowing out of. Granted, many times you only have one NIC, so this is obvious information, but what if you are working with a multi-homed server and you are simply checking to make sure packets for a particular destination are flowing out the correct NIC? What if we just want to double-check that some route statements we added are working properly? Cue `Pathping`. This command has been around for a long time but is virtually unknown. It shows the same information that `tracert` does, except it saves the information about the time between hops and some other details until the end of the output. This allows you to focus on the physical hops themselves in a clear, concise manner. More importantly, it shows you our key ingredient right away—the NIC that your packets are flowing out of! Once I discovered this, I left `tracert` behind and have never looked back. `Pathping` is the way to go.

Getting ready

Not much to get ready for this one. All we need is a server with a network connection and a Command Prompt window. `Pathping` is a command that is already available to any Windows Server; we just need to start using it.

How to do it...

The following two steps get you started with `Pathping`:

1. Open **Command Prompt** on your server

2. Type `pathping <servername or IP>`. Your output will be as follows:

```
Administrator: Command Prompt                                    —    □    ✕

C:\>pathping dc1

Tracing route to DC1.MYDOMAIN.LOCAL [10.0.0.1]
over a maximum of 30 hops:
  0   WEB1.MYDOMAIN.LOCAL [10.0.0.85]
  1   DC1 [10.0.0.1]

Computing statistics for 25 seconds...
            Source to Here   This Node/Link
Hop  RTT    Lost/Sent = Pct  Lost/Sent = Pct  Address
  0                                            WEB1.MYDOMAIN.LOCAL [10.0.0.85]
                                0/ 100 =  0%   |
  1    0ms     0/ 100 =  0%    0/ 100 =  0%   DC1 [10.0.0.1]

Trace complete.

C:\>
```

How it works...

`Pathping` is a networking tool that allows you to watch the path that your packets are taking as they make their way to the destination. Similar to traceroute, it is much less commonly known, but in my opinion gives a better layout of the same data. It is a command that should be added to your regular tool bag and vocabulary, right alongside `ping` and `telnet`.

Setting up NIC Teaming

Teaming your network cards basically means installing two NICs onto the same server, plugging them both into the same network, and joining them together in a *team*. This gives you NIC redundancy in case of a failure, and redundancy is always a great thing! Sounds simple, right? Well, with Windows Server 2016, it finally is. This seemingly easy task has always been challenging to put into practice with previous versions of the operating system, but with 2016 we can finally do it properly from a single interface and actually count on it to work as we expect it to.

Getting ready

We are going to set up a NIC team on a Windows Server 2016 machine. There are two NICs installed onto this server, neither of which have yet been configured.

How to do it...

With the following steps, start teaming up:

1. Open up **Server Manager**, and in the left-hand pane go ahead and click on **Local Server**.
2. Near the middle of the screen, you will see a section marked **NIC Teaming**. Go ahead and click on the word **Disabled** in order to launch the NIC Teaming screen as follows:

Windows Firewall	Domain: On
Remote management	Enabled
Remote Desktop	Disabled
NIC Teaming	Disabled
NIC1	IPv4 address assigned by DHCP, IPv6 enabled
NIC2	IPv4 address assigned by DHCP, IPv6 enabled

3. Down in the **TEAMS** section, drop down the **TASKS** menu, and click on **New Team**:

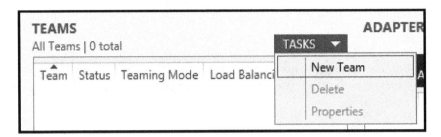

4. Define a name for your new team and choose the two NICs that you want to be a part of it:

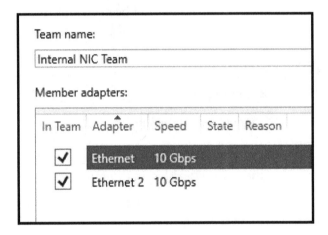

5. That's it! NIC1 and NIC2 are now successfully joined together in a team and will work in tandem to make sure you are still connected in the event of a failure.

6. If you make your way to the regular **Network Connections** screen, where you define IP address information, you will see that you now have a new item listed beneath your physical network cards. This new item is the place where you will go to define the IP address information that you want the server to use:

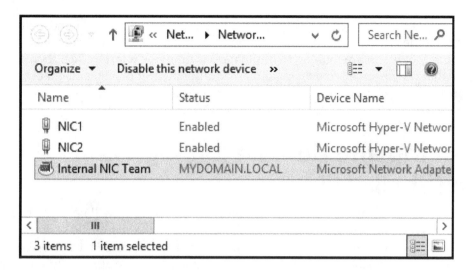

You can create more than one team on a server! When setting up a multi-homed server with two network connections, you could easily make use of four NICs and create two teams, each containing two physical network cards.

How it works...

Creating NIC teams is a pretty easy process that you should practice as time permits. This option for redundancy has never been very popular because, I believe, it had some stability problems in earlier versions of the server operating systems. Now that we have Windows Server 2016 available to us, and the process to configure it is so straightforward, I fully expect that NIC Teaming will become a standard procedure for administrators as they build every new server.

Another benefit of, and reason for, setting up NIC teaming is additional bandwidth. This may be yet another reason for which you start setting up your own servers with NIC teams. Keep in mind that if you are looking to implement teaming on a large scale, there is a limit of 32 NICs that can be joined to a team, and an additional limit of 32 teams that can be created on a single server.

Renaming and domain joining via PowerShell

Every server that you build will need a hostname, and most likely will need to be joined to your domain. We are all familiar with doing these things with the mouse using system properties, but have you ever thought of using a command interface to do these tasks quickly? Let's work together to discover how PowerShell can once again help make these necessary tasks more efficient.

Getting ready

We have just finished turning on a new Windows Server 2016 machine. Immediately following the mini-setup wizard in order to get logged into Windows, let's now use PowerShell to set our hostname and join the system to our domain.

How to do it...

Follow these steps to rename and domain join this new server with PowerShell:

1. Right-click on your PowerShell icon on the Taskbar and choose **Run as Administrator**:

2. In order to rename our new server WEB2, input the following command. Using the -Restart flag will ensure that our server reboots following the name change:

```
Rename-Computer -NewName WEB2 -Restart
```

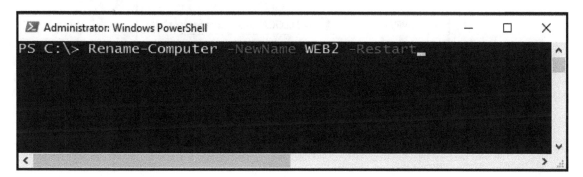

3. That's it for renaming! Now that our WEB2 server has rebooted, open PowerShell again and use the `Add-Computer` command in order to join it to our domain:

```
Add-Computer -DomainName MYDOMAIN.LOCAL -Credential
    MYDOMAIN.LOCAL\Administrator -Restart
```

4. Since we specified an account to use as credentials when joining the domain, we are prompted to supply the password. As soon as you enter the password, the server will be joined to the domain and will immediately restart to complete the process:

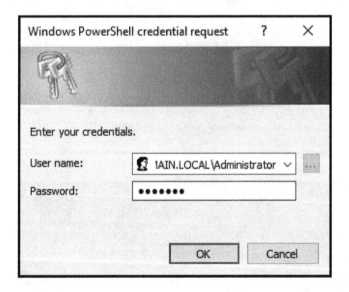

5. Following the reboot, you can see in system properties that our server is now appropriately named and domain joined:

```
Computer name, domain, and workgroup settings
    Computer name:          WEB2
    Full computer name:     WEB2.MYDOMAIN.LOCAL
    Computer description:
    Domain:                 MYDOMAIN.LOCAL
```

How it works...

Through a couple of quick PowerShell cmdlets, we can rename computers and join them to our domain. In fact, these functions are even possible without ever logging into the console of the server. There are parameters that can be added to these cmdlets that allow you to run them remotely. For example, you could run the PowerShell commands from a local desktop computer, specifying that you want to run them against the remote server's IP address or name. By performing the functions this way, you never even have to log into the server itself in order to name and join it. See the links in the following section for additional information on these parameters.

See also

Take a look at the following links for even more detailed information about the Rename-Computer and Add-Computer cmdlets that we used in this recipe:

- http://technet.microsoft.com/en-us/library/hh849792.aspx
- http://technet.microsoft.com/en-us/library/hh849798.aspx

Building your first Server Core

Perhaps the most important way to increase security in your organization is to lower the security threshold, or footprint, of your servers and infrastructure. In other words, if there are any services running or ports open on your servers that aren't actually being used purposefully, you should disable or turn that particular service off. Now, hardening a Windows Server by disabling services and uninstalling things isn't an easy job; you can quickly turn something off that is important to the operating system and cause all kinds of problems on that server. Thankfully, there is a much safer and more secure way to harden your servers, but it requires planning from the beginning of your server build.

Server Core is a version of Windows Server 2016 that is essentially a headless operating system; all of your interaction with it is either command-line driven or done remotely from other servers or systems. Server Core is an alternate installation method to the full Windows desktop version of Server 2016. It installs the necessary technical componentry to behave as a Windows Server, join to your domain, and host the roles and services you need it to host, but it does all of that without a graphical desktop interface. This dramatically lowers the security vulnerability footprint and attack vectors on the server, but does mean you have to re-wire your brain in how you interact with these servers. Since Server Core is a big leap forward for security in many companies, it is appropriate that we start working with it here in our chapter regarding security. Let's take a quick look at the installation process for it, and an initial glance at the interface, so you get familiar with the console you will be looking at on these new, hardened servers you are going to start using.

Getting ready

We are going to build a new instance of Windows Server 2016 but will be making sure to choose the appropriate options for installing Server Core and not the full desktop experience version of the operating system. Our new server will be a VM; it doesn't have to be actual hardware.

How to do it...

Here is a procedure that will get you started rolling out your first instance of Windows Server 2016, Server Core:

1. Create your new VM—or physical server—and insert the Windows Server 2016 installation media, just like you would if you were installing the full version of the operating system. Walk through the installation steps, the only difference being that you want to make sure and choose the default option for **Windows Server 2016 Standard**. Or you can, of course, choose the Datacenter installation option, but the important part here is that you do *NOT* choose the **(Desktop Experience)** version of the operating system, as that would give us a regular old desktop interface just like any other server. By choosing the top option, and notice that it is now the default installation option, we are telling it that we want the more secure Server Core version of Windows Server 2016:

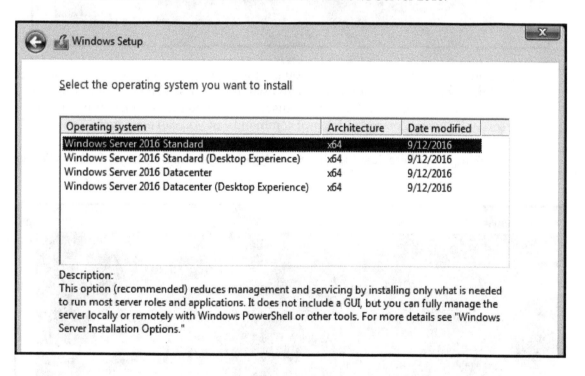

2. Finish walking through the installation wizard, and when your new server has booted, instead of being presented with the standard Windows mini-setup wizard in order to start configuring your server, you will simply be presented with the following screen:

3. Upon pressing *Ctrl + Alt + Delete* you are prompted to set a password for the local administrator account, after which you will find yourself sitting at a traditional Command Prompt interface. From this interface, you can interact with your new server by using Command Prompt commands, or you can even type powershell in order to move over into the PowerShell interface and start working from there, just like you would with PowerShell on any Windows Server 2016:

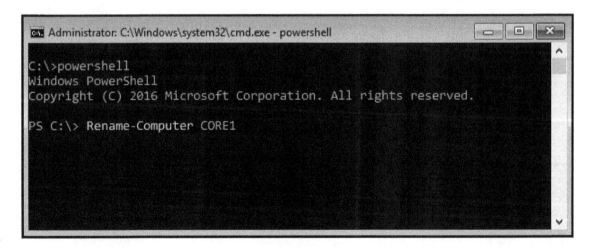

4. The Server Core Shell is not limited to command-line interfacing. If you were to type notepad.exe and press *Enter*, the Notepad application will appear, within which you can utilize your mouse as well as the keyboard:

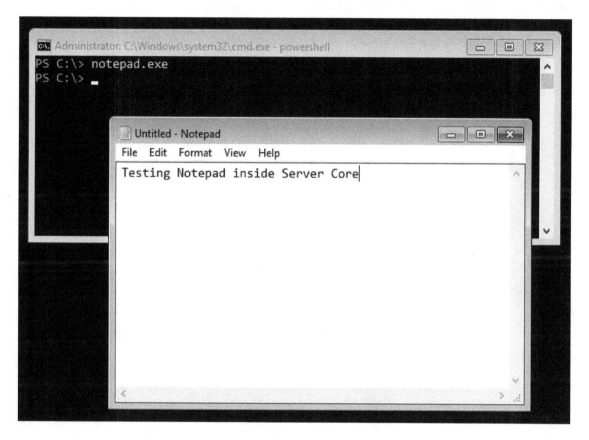

5. From this point, the most common tasks are going to be the same as the things you would do in a desktop experience version of Windows Server 2016. You can use the Command Prompt or PowerShell interfaces to set IP addresses, set a hostname for your server, and even join it to your domain. There are cmdlets that will allow you to install the Windows roles that you need to run on this server as well.

How it works...

Microsoft would like headless servers to be the way of the future, and it is critical that server administrators know this technology exists, and start to use it in their day-to-day server workloads. A quick recipe in order to get the operating system up and running is a good start, but working with Server Core regularly and learning the common commands that you will need to use is essential information to really get started interacting with these headless versions of the operating system. Server Core can be an enormous security benefit; all you need to do is start using it!

Working with Certificates

2

Understanding certificates is something that I avoided for many years in my technology career. For many facets of IT, you never had to deal with them. That was for the networking guys, not anybody doing development or desktop support. Times have changed, and a solid understanding of the common certificate types is quickly becoming an ability that anyone in support should possess. More and more security is becoming focused on certificates, and with the exponential increase in the amount of applications that are served via the Web, understanding the certificates that protect these services is more important than ever.

Almost anyone who has set up a website has dealt with SSL certificates from a public **certification authority (CA)**, but did you know that you can be your own CA? That you can issue certificates to the machines in your network right from your own CA server? Follow along as we explore some of the capabilities of Windows Server 2016 running as a CA server in your network. Our work in this chapter will cover the following topics:

- Setting up the first certification authority server in a network
- Building a Subordinate certification authority server
- Creating a certificate template to prepare for issuing machine certificates to your clients
- Publishing a certificate template to allow enrollment
- Using MMC to request a new certificate
- Using the web interface to request a new certificate
- Configuring Autoenrollment to issue certificates to all domain joined systems
- Renewing your root certificate

Introduction

When getting to know a new customer and network as part of my day job, I generally find that one of two things are true. Either they don't have a CA server, or they do, but it isn't being used for anything yet. Most folks know that certificates are upcoming and in demand and that new technologies are released all the time that require a fairly large use of certificates. Technologies such as Lync (Skype for Business), SharePoint, System Center, DirectAccess, or even just building a website almost always require the use of a certificate in today's world. Jumping into a project to deploy almost any new system these days will quickly bring you to the realization that a knowledge of certificates is becoming mandatory. Even in places where they aren't required, they are usually still recommended in order to make the solution more secure or to adhere to best practices.

Together, we are going to build a **public key infrastructure** (**PKI**) environment inside our network and use it for some common certificate issuing tasks. By the end of this chapter, you should be comfortable with creating a PKI in your own environment, which will prepare you for any requirements you may encounter when working with certificate-based technologies.

Setting up the first certification authority server in a network

The first hurdle to overcome when you want to start certificate work is putting the server into place. There are many valid questions to be answered. Do I need a dedicated server for this task? Can I co-locate this role on an existing server? Do I need to install an Enterprise or stand-alone CA? I've heard the term offline root, but what does that mean? Let's start with the basics and assume that you need to build the first CA server in your environment.

In an AD domain network, the most useful CA servers are of the Enterprise variety. Enterprise CA servers integrate with AD, making them visible to machines in the network and automatically trusted by computers that you join to your domain. There are differing opinions on the matter of best practices when setting up a series of CA servers. For example, there is a good test lab guide (referenced at the end of this recipe) published by Microsoft, which walks you through setting up a stand-alone Root CA, a Subordinate Enterprise CA, and then taking the stand-alone root offline. An advantage of this is that certificates are issued from the subordinate, not directly from the root, and so if certificate keys are somehow compromised in the environment, the Root CA is completely offline and unavailable so that it cannot be compromised. In this situation, you could wipe out the subordinate and the certificates it has published, bring up the offline root, build out a new subordinate, and be back in business publishing certificates without having to regenerate a new Root CA server.

Given the preceding best practice, or as defined by some anyway, it is surprising that I quite rarely see offline Root CAs in the field. Almost never, in fact. And in some of the cases where I have, the existence of an offline Root CA has caused problems. Just as an example, when deploying a DirectAccess infrastructure with **one-time-password** (OTP) capabilities in a customer environment, it was discovered that in order to make the OTP work correctly, the offline Root CA had to be brought back online. This wasn't in the best interests of the way the PKI had been established, and so instead we had to implement a second certificate environment to be a stand-alone root with two intermediaries in order to maintain an online Root CA for the purpose of the OTP certificates. This caused big delays in the project, as we had to build the three new servers necessary just to get the certificates published in the correct way, which caused a much more complex certificate infrastructure to support afterward.

If the preceding description confused you, good—because it's kind of a messy setup. If the company had instead been running on the online Root CA server in the first place, none of this extra work would have been necessary. I'm not advocating that an Enterprise Root CA that remains online all the time is the best way to do certificates, but it will cause you the fewest problems, and there are many companies that operate their production CA environments in exactly this way.

Another field observation is that most small- or medium-sized companies do not take the offline Root CA approach. In fact, I find that many small businesses need to co-host servers in order to save resources and have their CA role installed onto a server that is also performing some other task. Many times, the CA role is installed onto a domain controller. While at the surface level this appears to make sense, because the Enterprise CA services are so tightly integrated with AD, it is actually a bad idea. Microsoft recommends that you never co-host the CA role onto a domain controller, so stay away from that scenario if you can. That being said, I have seen dozens of companies that do exactly this and have never had a problem with it, so I suppose it's just your call on how closely you want to adhere to the *Microsoft way*. Make sure to do some reading from the links provided at the end of this recipe, as they should provide you with information that is helpful to make the right decisions about which certificate server setup is best suited for your network.

Getting ready

I have created a new Windows Server 2016 named CA1, a domain member upon which we will be enabling our new certificate infrastructure.

How to do it...

To install Active Directory Certificate Services onto your Server 2016, use the following set of instructions:

1. Open **Server Manager** and click the **Add roles and features** link.
2. Walk through the steps, choosing the default settings. When you come to the **Server Roles** screen, select **Active Directory Certificate Services**.
3. Upon selecting the role, you will be prompted to confirm the installation of additional features. Go ahead and click on **Add Features**:

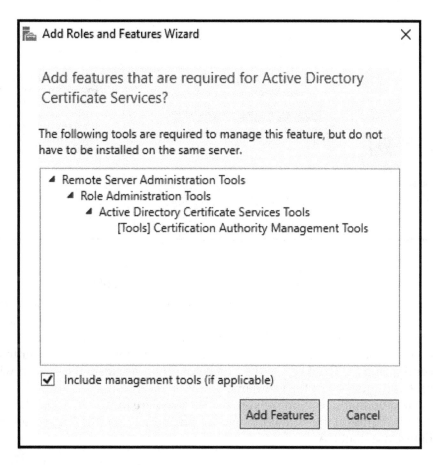

4. Click **Next** a couple of times until you come to the **Role Services** screen. Here you will see a few different options that can be used on your CA server. Since we would like to be able to request certificates from a web interface on the CA, I am going to check the additional box for **Certification Authority Web Enrollment**. After selecting this box, you will receive an additional pop-up box asking you to add features. Make sure to allow those features to be installed:

Select the role services to install for Active Directory Certificate Services

Before You Begin	**Role services**		**Description**
Installation Type			
Server Selection	☑ Certification Authority		Certification Authority Web Enrollment provides a simple Web
Server Roles	☐ Certificate Enrollment Policy Web Service		interface that allows users to
Features	☐ Certificate Enrollment Web Service		perform tasks such as request and
	☑ Certification Authority Web Enrollment		renew certificates, retrieve certificate
AD CS	☐ Network Device Enrollment Service		revocation lists (CRLs), and enroll for
Role Services	☐ Online Responder		smart card certificates.
Web Server Role (IIS)			
Role Services			
Confirmation			
Results			

5. Click **Next** through the remaining screens until you reach the last page, where you click on the **Install** button to start the installation of the role.

6. Once completed, you will see a link inside your installation summary screen that says **Configure Active Directory Certificate Services on the destination server**. You can click either on this link or on the Server Manager notifications yellow exclamation mark near the top of the Server Manager screen in order to continue configuring the CA role. On the first configuration screen, the wizard will probably auto-insert the username of the currently logged-in user. As stated in the text on that screen, make sure the user you are logged in as has Enterprise Admin rights on the domain, as we are planning to set this CA server up as an Enterprise Root CA.

You can click on **More about AD CS Server Roles** at any time to read more information about the different types of CA roles and features available. For the purposes of this recipe, we will not discuss them all, but rather focus on creating our Enterprise Root CA.

7. To get certificate services rolling on our server, go ahead and check the top two options to configure **Certification Authority** and **Certification Authority Web Enrollment**:

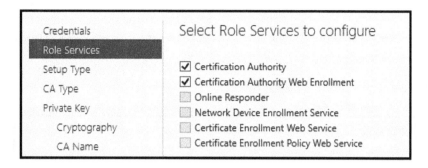

8. Choose **Enterprise CA**.
9. Choose **Root CA;** because this is our first CA server, we need to implement a root before we can think about a subordinate.
10. Choose **Create a new private key**.
11. On the **Cryptography** screen, you have the ability to choose the kind of crypto options you can provide on your CA server. Typically, the default options will work best if you're unsure of these settings. Just make sure that the **Key length** field is set to **2048** as a minimum. This is the new industry standard for the minimum key length. Similarly, hash standards have changed recently to SHA256, you should really no longer be using SHA1 for any of your certificates as it has now been estimated that SHA1 could be compromised in the next couple of years:

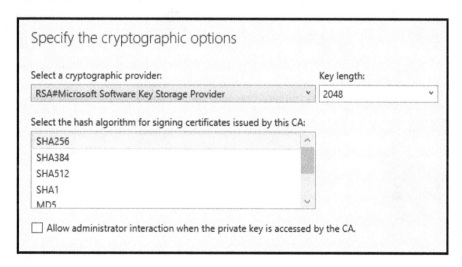

12. If desired, you may modify the **Common name for this CA**. Keep in mind, this does not have to match the hostname of the server in any way. This is the name of the CA that will show up inside Active Directory as well as inside the certificates that you issue from this CA. Typically, I find that admins leave the **Distinguished name suffix** field alone:

Common name for this CA:

MyDomain-CertServer

Distinguished name suffix:

DC=MYDOMAIN,DC=LOCAL

Preview of distinguished name:

CN=MyDomain-CertServer,DC=MYDOMAIN,DC=LOCAL

13. Change the **Validity Period** of your root certificate if desired. Often admins blow through this screen and leave it set at the default five years, but that means in just five short years you will suddenly invalidate every single certificate that you have ever issued from this CA server. I recommend increasing that number to 10 or even 20 years so you don't have to worry about this level of certificate expiry for a long time. The validity period will determine how often the root certificate has to be renewed.

14. Continue through the remaining screens, leaving the default options set in place. When this wizard finishes, your CA server is now live.

15. It is generally a good idea to schedule a reboot for this server after such a significant role installation. Go ahead and reboot when time permits:

The following roles, role services, or features were configured:

∧ **Active Directory Certificate Services**

Certification Authority   ✓ **Configuration succeeded**
More about CA Configuration

Certification Authority Web Enrollment   ✓ **Configuration succeeded**
More about Web Enrollment Configuration

How it works...

In this recipe, we installed the first CA server into our network. As we discussed, you will want to make sure you read over some of the following links to help determine how many CAs you require and where they should be installed. This is one of those answers that can be different for every organization, and so I cannot make any blanket statements here that will apply for everyone. You may decide that your primary Root CA should be stand-alone rather than enterprise, and that is fine as long as it fits your needs. We also installed the web services piece of the role onto our primary CA because we plan to use this in upcoming recipes to issue certificates. If you are building an environment with multiple CA servers, you might determine that your root authority doesn't need the web interface...maybe only a particular subordinate CA will do that job for you. There are numerous ways that our design could play out, but through this recipe, I hope that enough information is provided so that you are comfortable with the actual process once those decisions have been made.

There are a couple of items that we did not cover in this recipe that should be pointed out. Following the preceding steps will get you a CA server up and running that is ready to issue certificates, there is no doubt about that. The remainder of the recipes in this chapter reflect CAs built exactly as shown here. However, there are additional steps that can be taken in order to further customize your CA settings if you have the need. If you plan to issue SSL certificate for websites, especially if you plan to install these certificates onto web servers which are facing the Internet, then you need to familiarize yourself with the **Certificate Revocation List** (**CRL**) settings. Whenever a certificate is accessed, the client computer checks in with the CRL in order to make sure the certificate is still valid. If the certificate is not valid or is fraudulent in some way, the CRL check will identify that compromise and disallow the connection. Particularly when publishing websites to the Internet that use certificates issued by your internal PKI, you will need to plan the publishing of your CRL so that external client computers can access it in a clean, secure fashion. Here is a great link to get you started on CRL information: `http://technet.microsoft.com/en-us/library/cc771079.aspx`.

The second piece of information I would like to reference is the CAPolicy.inf file. This is a file that can be populated with various customization settings for your CA server, such as the validity period of your root certificate, information about your CRL, and whether or not you want the default certificate templates to be loaded during CA role installation. If any of these settings are of interest to you, you simply create a CAPolicy.inf file with the appropriate configurations and place it inside C:\Windows on your CA server prior to role installation. The role installation wizard will then utilize the settings inside this file during role installation and incorporate your customizations. If you do not use one of these files, it is fine, and the role will be installed with some default settings in place just like we did in this recipe. But if you are interested in changing some of them, check out this link for more detailed information on the CAPolicy.inf file: http://technet.microsoft.com/en-us/library/jj125373.aspx.

Neither of these items, tweaking the CRL or using a CAPolicy.inf file, are required in order to get a certificate environment up and running. Thus, they are not included in the step-by-step configuration of the recipe itself. But I am always a fan of having all knowledge available to me on a particular subject, and so I strongly encourage you to read over these additional links provided to round out your understanding of possible functionality.

See also

Here are some links that make for good additional reading on this subject. In order to make an informed decision about what sequence of CA servers is right for your environment, I encourage you to do as much reading on the subject as possible before proceeding in the production network:

- http://technet.microsoft.com/en-us/library/dn786443.aspx
- http://technet.microsoft.com/en-us/library/dn786436.aspx
- http://technet.microsoft.com/en-us/library/hh831348.aspx

Building a Subordinate certification authority server

We build Subordinate CAs not really for the purposes of redundancy, like with many other kinds of servers, but because there are specific tasks that you may want to perform on a subordinate CA rather than a Root CA. If you issue a lot of certificates or different kinds of certificates, you may want to differentiate between CA servers when issuing. Perhaps you want machine certificates that are used for IPsec to be issued from IPSEC-CA, but the SSL website certificates that you issue should show as being issued from WEB-CA. Rather than building out two independent Root CAs that both have top-level rights, you should consider creating a single Root CA, maybe called ROOT-CA, and placing these two CA servers in a subordinate role under the Root CA in the chain. This can also be useful for geographically dispersed networks, having Subordinate CA servers dedicated to assigning certificates for different offices or regions.

As we discussed in the previous recipe, there are certainly some best practice standards that would suggest you only utilize Subordinate CAs to accomplish your certificate issuance. I don't always find that this is feasible for companies, particularly smaller ones, but it is a good idea if you can swing it. With Subordinate CA servers online, you have the option of bringing your Root CA offline, and using the Subordinates to issue all of your certificates.

Getting ready

We are inside a domain network and have a single Enterprise Root CA online and running. We now require an additional server that will be joined to the CA environment as a new Subordinate CA.

How to do it...

To implement our new Subordinate CA server, the process will be very similar to the *Setting up the first certification authority server in a network* recipe. However, there are a few key differences, and that is where we will focus. Some of the specific steps may be shortened here; please refer the previous recipe for more detailed information on the specific steps and settings with regards to installation of the role:

1. Log in to our new server, which has already been joined to the domain.

2. Follow the steps to add the Active Directory Certificate Services role to this server.

3. When we implemented our Root CA server, we chose to install the web services as well. This will enable us to request and issue certificates from a browser inside our network. You have the option of installing these web services on the new Subordinate CA, which you would definitely do if you planned on using an offline Root CA, but for our situation, we are not going to do this. We will stick with only **Certification Authority** in our list of available role services:

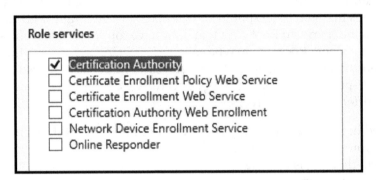

4. After the role has finished installing, go ahead and click on your link for **Configure Active Directory Certificate Services on the destination server**.

5. Input credentials as needed and choose the only option we have in the list to configure, **Certificate Authority**.

6. Here is where we start to detour from the path that we took with our Root CA creation. We are still choosing to set up an **Enterprise CA** because we still want it to be domain-integrated:

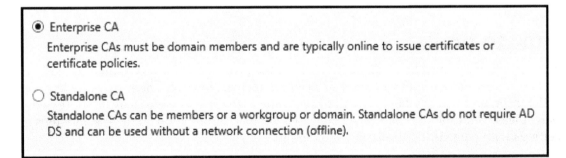

7. But instead of choosing to install a new Root CA, we are going to choose the option for **Subordinate CA**. In fact, it was already chosen for us as the default, because it recognizes that a Root CA already exists in the network. We could install another Root CA, but that is not our purpose in this recipe:

○ Root CA

Root CAs are the first and may be the only CAs configured in a PKI hierarchy.

◉ Subordinate CA

Subordinate CAs require an established PKI hierarchy and are authorized to issue certificates by the CA above them in the hierarchy.

8. Choose **Create a new private key**. The only time we would typically want to use an existing private key is when rebuilding a CA server.
9. Choose your cryptography settings. These are typically going to be the same that you configured on the Root CA.
10. Name your new Subordinate CA appropriately. If you have a specific function in mind for this CA, it will be helpful to you in the future to name it accordingly. For example, I intend to use this subordinate CA to issue all of the SSL certificates that I will need for internal webpages, so I have included *SSL* in the name:

Common name for this CA:

MyDomain-SSLCertServer

11. Now we come to a new screen. We need to acquire a certificate from our parent CA server in order to issue certificates from this new one. Choose the option for **Send a certificate request to a parent CA**, and use the **Select...** button to choose your Root CA:

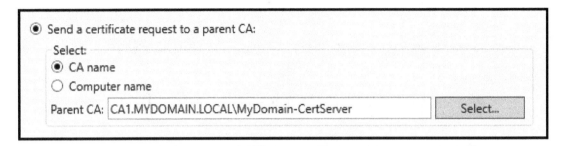

12. On the following screen, adjust the location of the certificate database files if required; otherwise, click **Next**, then **Configure**.

How it works...

Installing a Subordinate CA server in a network is very similar to implementing our first Root CA server. In our case, we simplified the installation by not having the requirement for the web services to run on the Subordinate, we will do all of those requests from the Root CA. We now have a Root CA running and a Subordinate CA running under it. For our installation, we are going to leave both online and running as we intend to issue certificates from both. We could easily run through this same process again with another new server in order to create another Subordinate CA, maybe to issue a different kind of certificate or for a different division of the company to utilize.

See also

- The *Setting up the first certification authority server in a network* recipe.

Creating a certificate template to prepare for issuing machine certificates to your clients

This recipe is the first hurdle that many new certificate admins bump into. You may have a CA server up and running, but what's next? Before you can start granting certificates to computers and users, you need to establish certificate templates that you are going to publish. You will configure these templates with particular settings, and when a certificate is requested against the template, that new certificate will be built based on the information in the template combined with the information provided by the certificate requestor.

There are some built-in certificate templates that preinstall when you add the CA role to your server. Some companies utilize these built-in templates for issuing certificates, but it is a better practice to create your own templates. There is no need to start from scratch, though. You can take one of the built-in templates, find one that comes close to meeting your needs, and tweak it to do your bidding with your particular certificate needs. This is the process we are going to be taking. We need to issue machine certificates to each of our systems in the network to authenticate some IPsec tunnels. There are a few criteria we need to meet in these certificates, and the built-in Computer template comes close to checking all the options that we need. So we will take that template, copy it, and modify it to meet our requirements.

Getting ready

This is a Server 2016 domain environment with a new CA server running. We will utilize the CA console on our CA server to accomplish this work today. The new template that we create will be automatically replicated with other CA servers in the domain.

How to do it...

The following steps will help you build a new certificate template:

1. Launch the **Certification Authority** management tool from inside Server Manager.
2. Expand the name of your CA and click on **Certificate Templates**. You will see a list of the built-in templates available to us.
3. Right-click on **Certificate Templates** and choose **Manage**:

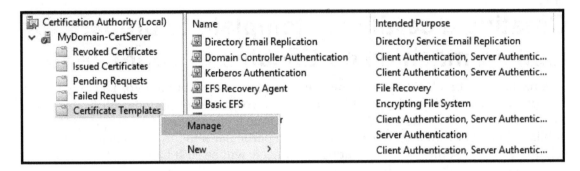

4. Right-click on the **Computer** template and choose **Duplicate Template**:

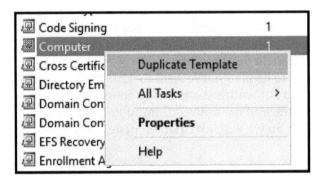

5. Now we adjust options within the certificate template. Any attributes that your certificates must have, you set here in the template properties. As an example, let's configure a few items that our new IPsec certificates must contain to be valid.

6. Go to the **General** tab and set the **Template display name** so that you can identify this new template we are building:

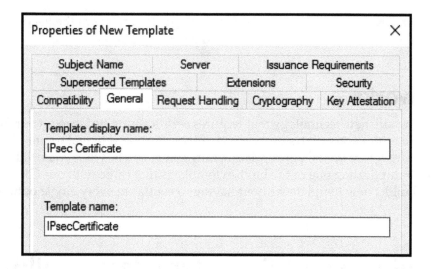

7. On the same tab, adjust the **Validity period** field to 2 years.

8. Browse to the **Subject Name** tab and set **Common name** as the **Subject name format** field. This will cause the subject name of the certificate to reflect the hostname of the computer that is requesting the certificate. Using the DNS name as the alternate subject name is another requirement that we have been given for our new certificates. You can see it checked in the screenshot below. Since we used the built-in Computer template as our starting point, this checkbox, as well as other requirements that we needed covered, were already taken care of for us:

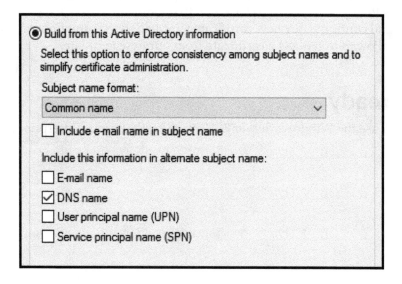

9. Click **OK**. There is now a brand new certificate template in the list called `IPsec Certificate` (or whatever name you gave to yours).

How it works...

When installing any new technology that requires certificates to be issued, your first stop should be the certificate templates on your CA server. You need to make sure that you have a template configured with the appropriate settings and switches that you need in your new certificates. By duplicating one of the built-in templates that came with our CA server, we were able to build a new template without having to configure every single option from the ground up.

Publishing a certificate template to allow enrollment

One of the most common certificate troubleshooting tasks I encounter is figuring out why a particular certificate template is not available when the user or computer tries to request a certificate. Having created a new certificate template does not necessarily mean that you are ready to start issuing certificates based on that template. We also need to publish our new template so that the CA server knows that it is ready to publish out to computers and users. There is also a security section of the template properties, where you need to define who or what has access to request certificates based on that template. In this recipe, we will find those settings and configure our new certificate template so that any domain joined workstation is allowed to request a certificate from our new template.

Getting ready

We are going to use the Windows Server 2016 machine that is our Enterprise Root CA.

How to do it...

In order to issue certificates based on a particular template, we need to take steps to publish and adjust the security properties of that template:

1. Launch the **Certification Authority** management tool from inside Server Manager.
2. Expand the name of your CA server in the left-hand tree.
3. Right-click on **Certificate Templates** and navigate to **New | Certificate Template to Issue**:

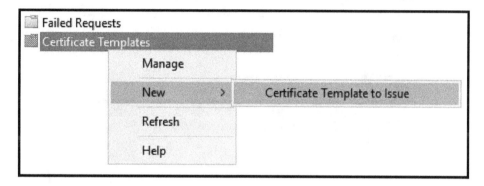

4. Select your new template from the list and click on **OK**.
5. Now right-click on **Certificate Templates** and choose **Manage**.
6. Find the template that you want to modify. For our recipe, we are modifying the new template called `IPsec Certificate`.
7. Right-click on the template and choose **Properties**.
8. Browse to the **Security** tab.

9. Now we need to set up permissions according to your requirements. For our particular example, we want to issue IPsec certificates to all domain joined computers so that they can later be used during IPsec negotiations inside our network. Therefore, in our permissions, we add **Domain Computers** and we check the box to allow **Enroll** permissions:

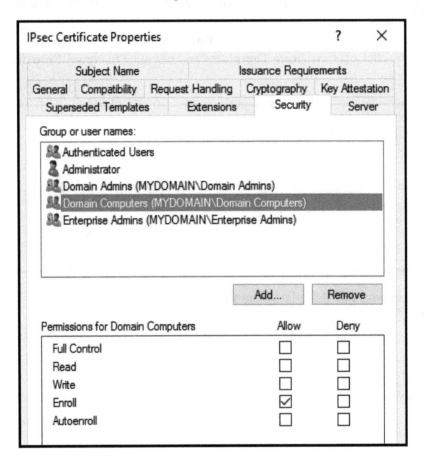

How it works...

A new certificate template doesn't do us any good without a couple of extra steps to publish that template. We need to walk through the process of specifying our new template to be issued, which is a simple option to accomplish but one that isn't immediately obvious inside the CA management console. Also, we need to make sure that the permissions we have set on our certificate template line up with the purpose for which our certificate is intended. If your user accounts are going to be requesting certificates, then you will have to add users or user groups and grant them enroll permissions. If computer accounts are going to be the ones making the requests, then make sure that the appropriate groups are entered in there with enrolling rights as well.

Using MMC to request a new certificate

The most common way that I see administrators interface with the certificates on their systems is through the MMC snap-in tool. **MMC** is short for **Microsoft Management Console**, and by using MMC, you can administer just about anything in the operating system. Though this is perhaps a greatly underutilized tool, I only generally see it being opened for a few select tasks. Requesting certificates is one of those tasks.

We are going to use the MMC console on a new server that we have in our network. There is a new certificate template that has been created, and we would like to issue one of these certificates to our new web server.

Getting ready

A Server 2016 Enterprise Root CA server is online and running in our network. On it, we have configured a new certificate template called IPsec Certificate. The steps have been taken to publish this template so that it may be requested from computers in our network. We are now working from a brand new web server that is also running Server 2016 and joined to our domain, where we are going to accomplish the work of manually requesting a certificate from the CA server.

How to do it...

Follow these steps to request a new certificate using the MMC console:

1. Open Command Prompt on our new web server and type mmc. Then press *Enter*. Alternatively, you could open MMC from the **Start** screen.

2. Now inside the MMC console, click on the **File** menu, then on **Add/Remove Snap-in...**.

3. Choose **Certificates** from the list of available snap-ins and click on the **Add** button. This will bring a new window with some more choices about the certificates snap-in.

4. First, we need to choose whether we are opening the user certificate repository or the Computer certificate repository. I don't generally see service account used in the field. The selection here will depend on what type of certificate you are requesting. For our example, we are looking for an IPsec certificate, which needs to go in the Computer container. Choose **Computer account** and click **Finish**:

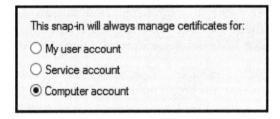

5. Leave the next option set on the **Local computer** and click **Finish** again.

6. Click **OK**.

7. There are also MSC launchers that can be utilized to bring you into the certificate stores even faster. Make use of these by navigating to **Start | Run** or Command Prompt and type the following commands:
   - CERTMGR.MSC opens user certificates
   - CERTLM.MSC opens computer certificates

8. Now back inside the main MMC console, expand **Certificates (Local Computer)** and select the Personal folder. You can see that there are currently no certificates installed here.

9. Right-click on the Personal folder and navigate to **All Tasks | Request New Certificate...**:

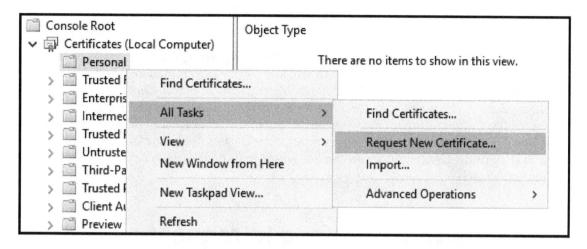

10. Click **Next**.

11. On the **Select Certificate Enrollment Policy** screen, **Active Directory Enrollment Policy** is automatically selected. Simply click **Next** again to go on to the next screen.

12. Now we see a list of certificate templates that are available to us. Check the boxes for the certificates that you want to request and click **Enroll**:

Active Directory Enrollment Policy		
☐ Computer	ⓘ **STATUS:** Available	Details ˅
☑ IPsec Certificate	ⓘ **STATUS:** Available	Details ˅

☐ Show all templates

If you are expecting to see a particular template here but it doesn't show up in the list, click on **Show all templates**. This will display a list of all templates on the CA server and give an explanation for each as to why it is not currently available. This can help for troubleshooting purposes.

How it works...

Utilizing the MMC console is a quick and easy way to request new certificates to be issued manually. In an Active Directory environment, any certificate template on the CA server that you have permissions to enroll will be visible and easy to enroll. Our example today displayed the enrollment process for a machine certificate that we are planning to use in the future for IPsec authentication. However, there are many cases where you may want to issue user-level certificates, rather than computer certificates. In those cases, you would want to snap-in the User account certificates, where in our example, we defined computer account certificates.

Using the web interface to request a new certificate

Sometimes when requesting a new certificate, you may not have access to query certificate services directly by using a tool such as the MMC snap-in. Or perhaps you want to provide a way for users to be able to request certificates even while outside the office. By enabling the web services portion of the CA role, we turn on a website that runs on our CA server. This website can be accessed from inside the corporate network and could potentially even be published out to the Internet with some kind of a reverse proxy solution.

For our recipe today, let's access the web interface that is now running on the CA server where we installed the web services part of the CA role. We will use this website to request and acquire a certificate on our client computer.

Getting ready

Our Enterprise Root CA is a Windows Server 2016 that has the Active Directory Certificate Services role installed. When we installed and configured the role, we made sure to select the option for the web service so that we could make use of it to request a new certificate.

How to do it...

We do not have to be logged into the CA server directly to accomplish this work. Instead, we are logged into a new web server in our environment. From this web server, we take the following steps:

1. Open Internet Explorer and browse to `https://<CAServerName>/CertSrv/`. In our case, it is `https://CA1/CertSrv/`:

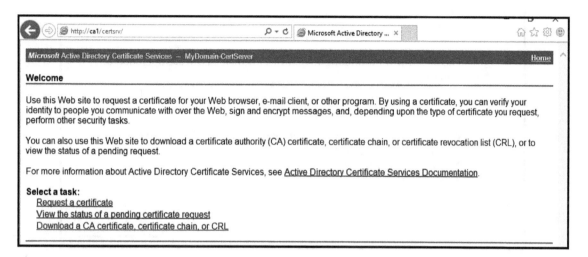

Make sure you specify to access the site using HTTPS or you will not be allowed to finish requesting a certificate later during the wizard.

2. Click on **Request a certificate**.
3. You will see there is a pre-built request in there for acquiring a user certificate. For one of those, you simply click on that link, then click Submit on the next screen. However, to dig a little deeper with our recipe, we are going to request an SSL certificate, not a user certificate. To start the process, click on **advanced certificate request**.
4. Choose **Create and submit a request to this CA**.

5. Click **Yes** if prompted with the following message:

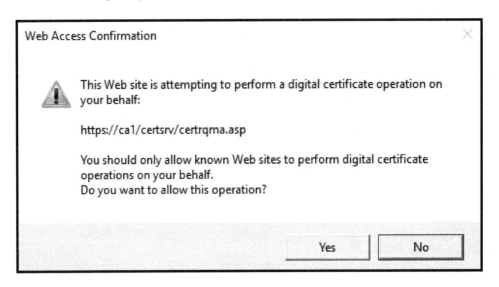

6. Choose the **Certificate Template** that you would like to use in order to accomplish your certificate request. On my Root CA server where the web services are installed, I set up a new template, which I duplicated from the Web Server template with my specific certificate requirements. I called this template **Custom Web Server** and have published it to be available for enrollment.

7. Because this is an SSL certificate, I need to populate the regularly requested information. My website name and company contact info is entered here.

8. The rest of the options available to change are already configured as I want them to be. This is because when I set up my Custom Web Server template, I already specified all of these item defaults. Here is my request:

Advanced Certificate Request

Certificate Template:

> Custom Web Server ⌄

Identifying Information For Offline Template:

Name: sharepoint.mydomain.local

E-Mail:

Company: Your Company name

Department: Web

City: YourCity

State: YourState

Country/Region: US

Key Options:

◉ Create new key set ○ Use existing key set

CSP: Microsoft RSA SChannel Cryptographic Provider ⌄

Key Usage: ◉ Exchange

Key Size: 2048 Min: 2048 Max:16384 (common key sizes: 2048 4096 8192 16384)

◉ Automatic key container name ○ User specified key container name

☑ Mark keys as exportable

☐ Enable strong private key protection

---

9. Click **Submit**.

10. Your browser will spin for a minute while the CA server creates the new certificate based on the information that you entered. When it is finished, you should have a link to click on called **Install this certificate**. Go ahead and click that link:

Microsoft Active Directory Certificate Services — MyDomain-CertServer

Certificate Installed

Your new certificate has been successfully installed.

How it works...

Running the web service on your CA server can be beneficial because it allows another method of requesting certificates. In this recipe, we were able to very quickly pull open our CA certificate requesting webpage and walk through some simple steps. This enabled us to download a new certificate that we are planning to use with our new web server's SharePoint site.

Because our web server is inside the corporate network, we could have also accomplished this request right from the Certificates MMC console. However, if our web server had been in a different building separated by networking equipment and firewalls, this may not have been an option for us. Or if we were trying to acquire a certificate from another machine that didn't have the MMC access for one reason or another, this web service is a nice way to accomplish the same task.

Configuring Autoenrollment to issue certificates to all domain joined systems

A lot of the new technologies requiring certificates to be used for authentication require those certificates to be distributed on a large scale. For example, if we want to use the Computer certificate for DirectAccess authentication, we need to issue a certificate to every DirectAccess client computer. This could be thousands of laptops in your network. If we want to start encrypting traffic inside the network with IPsec and require certificates to be distributed for that purpose, you would potentially need to issue some kind of machine certificate to every computer inside your network. While you could certainly issue each by hand using either the MMC console or the CA web interface, that doesn't sound like very much fun.

Enter **Autoenrollment**. We can turn on this feature, which is sort of like flipping a switch in Active Directory, and in doing so we can tell AD to issue certificates automatically to the computers, even if we need to get them to every single domain joined the system. Let's work together through this recipe to turn on this option and test it out.

Getting ready

We are working inside a Windows Server 2016 based Active Directory domain. We also have a Server 2016 Enterprise Root CA running in this network. The work that we will be accomplishing is a combination of work on the CA server and work inside Group Policy on a domain controller.

How to do it...

To enable Autoenrollment in your domain, take a look at these instructions:

1. Log into your CA server and open up **Certification Authority**. Expand the name of your CA, then right-click on **Certificate Templates** and choose **Manage**.
2. Now choose which certificate template that you want to be set up for Autoenrollment. I have a template called **DA Cert** that I want issued to every computer in my network. Right-click on **DA Cert** and head into **Properties**.

3. Click on the **Security** tab. Here you need to configure whatever users, computers, or other objects that you want to have Autoenroll permissions to this template. I am going to **Allow** the **Autoenroll** permission for all **Domain Computers** in my network, as shown in the following screenshot:

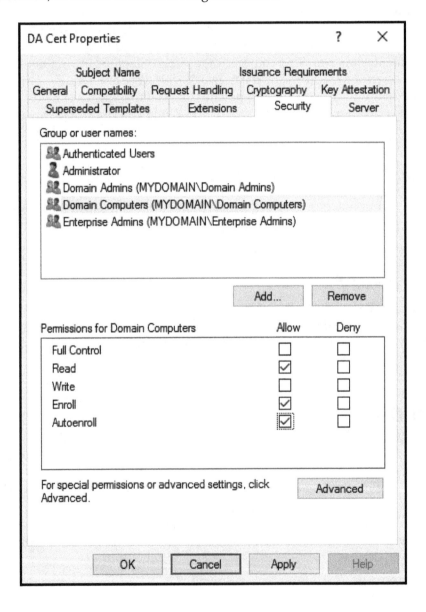

4. Click **OK**, and now we need to head over to Group Policy. Log into a domain controller and open the **Group Policy Management Console**.

5. I have created a new GPO for this task called **Certificate Autoenrollment Policy**. This new GPO is linked to the top of my domain so that it applies to all machines that are joined to the domain. If you didn't need your policy to be so broad, you could of course pare down the access here by limiting the link or filtering associated with your GPO.

6. Right-click on the **Certificate Autoenrollment Policy** GPO and choose **Edit...**:

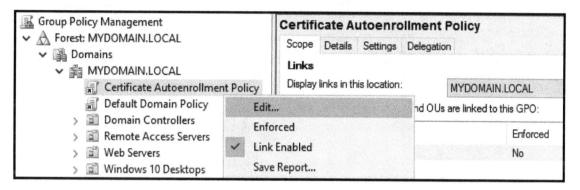

7. Navigate to **Computer Configuration** | **Policies** | **Windows Settings** | **Security Settings** | **Public Key Policies**.

8. Double-click on **Certificate Services Client - Auto-Enrollment**.

9. Set this to **Enabled**, and select both of the checkboxes on the screen:

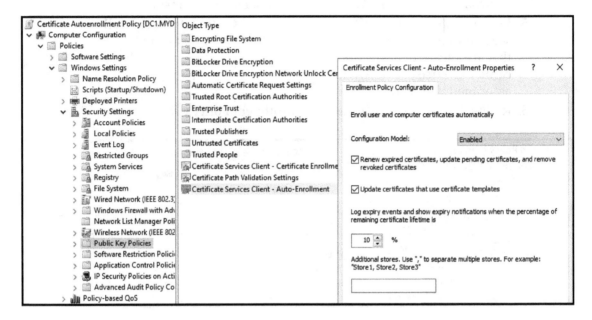

10. As soon as you click **OK**, this new GPO will start taking effect. Machines will check in with Group Policy and realize they need these new settings from the GPO. Upon putting this new option into place, the computers will then check in with the CA server and ask it for a copy of any certificate for which it has autoenroll permissions. Since we configured all Domain Computers to have autoenroll permission to our DA Cert template, our workstations and servers should immediately start receiving a copy of this new certificate. Here is a screenshot from my CA server just a few minutes after configuring this GPO. You can see that it is starting to issue certificates to my domain-joined systems:

7	MYDOMAIN\DC1$	-----BEGIN C...	Directory Email Repli...
8	MYDOMAIN\WEB1$	-----BEGIN C...	DA Cert (1.3.6.1.4.1.3...
9	MYDOMAIN\CA2$	-----BEGIN C...	DA Cert (1.3.6.1.4.1.3...

How it works...

We make use of Group Policy in order to flip our autoenrollment on-switch and immediately start the autoenrollment of certificates to our domain-joined systems. There are a couple of different ways that autoenrollment can be regulated. You can decide who gets the autoenrollment policy applied to them through Group Policy links and filtering, meaning that you can define in the GPO properties which users or computers are going to be subject to autoenrollment in the first place. Alternatively, or additionally, you can also specify permissions inside each certificate template on the CA server so that you can better determine which users or computers in your environment will receive copies of each template once autoenrollment is enabled.

Planning is essential to this task. You need to build a clear definition for what certificates you need to publish, and to which devices or people you need that certificate to roll itself out to. Follow the steps incorrectly and it may not work, or worse yet, you may end up with a thousand certificates being issued all over your network that you did not intend to be distributed. Group Policy is extremely powerful, and tapping into that power comes with great responsibility.

After configuring these settings, if you reboot a few domain joined machines in your network, you will notice that when they come back online, there will be a new certificate sitting in the computer's personal certificate store. Sit back and wait a few hours, and they will have rolled around to everybody automatically. If you don't like waiting for Group Policy to refresh, you can open Command Prompt on some of those computers and issue the `gpupdate /force` command to manually refresh the policies and pull down the certificate.

Renewing your root certificate

Remember a few pages back, when we configured the first CA server in our environment, the Enterprise Root? We left many of the default options in place, and that means that our root certificate is set automatically with a validity period of five years. This seems like a long time, but five years can flash by in an instant, especially if you have kids. So what happens when that root certificate finally does expire? Bad things happen. You will definitely want to keep track of the expiration date on your root certificates, and make sure to renew them before they expire!

Getting ready

We just built this new CA server, so we are not in danger of our root certificate expiring anytime soon. However, it is important to understand how to accomplish this task, so we are going to walk through the process of renewing the root authority certificate. We will accomplish this task right from our CA server itself.

How to do it...

To renew your CA's root certificate, take the following steps:

1. Log into the Enterprise Root CA server and open the **Certification Authority** management console.
2. Right-click on the name of your CA, navigate to **All Tasks** and then choose **Renew CA Certificate...**:

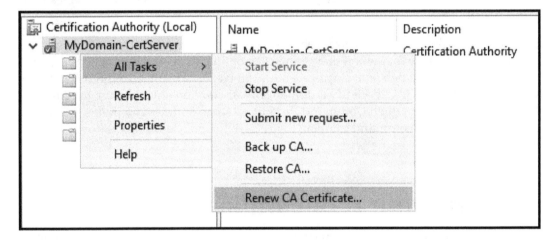

If you haven't stopped ADCS during this process, you will be prompted to do so. Go ahead and click **Yes** in order to stop the certificate processes temporarily.

3. On the **Renew CA Certificate** screen, you only have one option to worry about. You need to choose whether you want to generate a new key pair for the new root certificate or re-use the existing one. If you have published many certificates from this CA, it is generally easier to say **No** to this and let it re-use the existing key pair. As you can see on the screen, there are some situations where you would want to choose **Yes** and create a new key pair, so the correct answer to this question is going to depend on your situation and your needs:

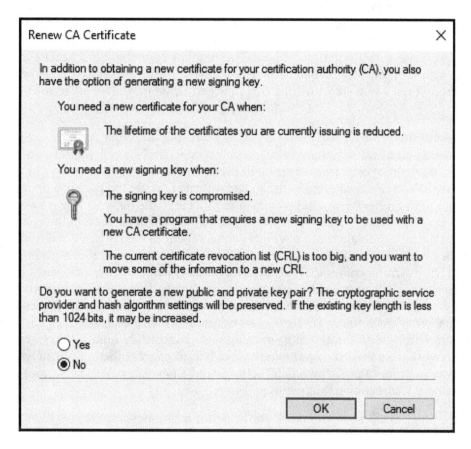

4. Click **OK**, and the new root certificate is immediately created and starts being distributed via Group Policy.

How it works...

Your top-level root certificate is critical to the overall health of your PKI infrastructure. If this certificate expires, every single certificate that has ever been issued from your CA servers will immediately become invalid. Fortunately, renewing this root certificate is generally pretty easy. Simply follow our steps and you're back in business for another 5 or 10 years. When you renew the root authority certificate, it places the new copy of that certificate into Group Policy's Trusted Root Authorities location. All systems joined to a domain keep this list updated automatically through Group Policy so that whenever you add a new CA server or renew an existing root certificate, the new trusts associated with that new certificate are automatically distributed to all of your client machines and servers. Therefore, generally, all you have to do is renew the certificate and sit back and relax, because Group Policy will start pushing that new certificate into place all across your network.

However—and this is a BIG however—if you let your root authority certificate expire and you have issued certificates that are being used by clients and servers for network authentication, the root certificate expiry will cause those systems to no longer be connected to the network. You can easily renew the root certificate and get the backend up and running, but without having a valid way to authenticate to the network, your systems that are relying on a valid certificate to connect to that network will be dead in the water. You will need to figure out an alternative way to connect them to the network and update their Group Policy before they will learn how to trust the newly refreshed root authority certificate. This warning comes to mind for me because I just helped a company combat exactly this issue. Their root certificate expired, and they had whole offices worth of people who were connecting to the data center and the domain solely through the DirectAccess remote connectivity technology. DirectAccess relies on certificates as part of its authentication process, so those remote systems were completely unable to communicate with the network once their root cert expired. We had to connect them to the network in a different way in order to pull down GPO settings and a new copy of the new root certificate before they could start connecting remotely again.

Moral of the story: make sure you mark your calendars to renew certificates BEFORE they expire!

3
Remote Access

With Windows Server 2016, Microsoft brings a whole new way of looking at remote access. Companies have historically relied on third-party tools to connect remote users to the network, such as traditional and SSL VPN provided by appliances from large networking vendors. I'm here to tell you those days are gone. Those of us running Microsoft-centric shops can now rely on Microsoft technologies to connect our remote workforce. Better yet is that these technologies are included with the Server 2016 operating system, and have functionality that is much improved over anything that a traditional VPN can provide.

Regular VPN does still have a place in the remote access space, and the great news is that you can also provide it with Server 2016. In fact, by now many of you have probably heard of a "new" remote access technology in Server 2016 called *Always On VPN*. I put the word *new* in quotes because the VPN technology on the server side has actually not changed at all, it is Windows 10 on the client side that has been adjusted to introduce this new way of creating VPN connections. In Windows Server 2016 (or any version of Windows Server), your setup procedures for Always On VPN are the same as any VPN access. When you look into whether or not you want to provide Always On VPN to your workforce, you are really exploring a client-side technology that was introduced in Windows 10 1709.

We have some recipes on setting up VPN, but our primary focus for this chapter will be **DirectAccess (DA)**. DA is kind of like *automatic VPN*. There is nothing the user needs to do in order to be connected to work. Whenever they are on the Internet, they are connected automatically to the corporate network. DirectAccess is an amazing way to have your Windows 7, Windows 8, and Windows 10 domain joined systems connected back to the network for data access and for the secure management of those traveling machines. DA has actually been around since 2008, but the first version came with some steep infrastructure requirements and was not widely used. Server 2016 brings a whole new set of advantages and makes implementation much easier than in the past.

There is currently a lot of confusion around the topics of DirectAccess and Always On VPN, and unfortunately many people are wondering if one is going to replace the other. Based on my experience and knowledge about how these things work, they actually supplement each other. When having discussions with customers about what remote access technology fits better into their environment, it's not always a matter of either/or, oftentimes it is *both*. DirectAccess definitely holds some advantages over AOVPN when you are talking about the best way to connect your domain-joined, corporate laptops. However, if you are interested in BYOD and providing users the ability to connect their personal computers or devices to your corporate network, that is where AOVPN can bring some functionality to the table that DA cannot. I still find many server and networking admins who have never heard of DirectAccess, so let's spend some time together exploring some of the common tasks associated with it.

In this chapter, we will cover the following recipes:

- DirectAccess planning question and answers
- Configuring DirectAccess, VPN, or a combination of the two
- Pre-staging Group Policy Objects to be used by DirectAccess
- Enhancing the security of DirectAccess by requiring certificate authentication
- Building your Network Location Server on its own system
- Enabling Network Load Balancing on your DirectAccess servers
- Adding VPN to your existing DirectAccess server
- Replacing your expiring IP-HTTPS certificate
- Reporting on DirectAccess and VPN connections

Introduction

There are two flavors of remote access available in Windows Server 2016. The most common way to implement the Remote Access role is to provide DirectAccess for your Windows 7, 8, and 10 domain-joined client computers, and VPN for the rest. The DA machines are typically your company-owned corporate assets. One of the primary reasons why DirectAccess is usually only for company assets is that the client machines must be joined to your domain because the DA configuration settings are brought down to the client through a GPO. I doubt you want the home and personal computers joining your domain.

VPN is therefore used for down-level clients or non-domain-joined Windows 7/8/10, and for home and personal devices that want to access the network. Since this is a traditional VPN listener with all regular protocols available such as PPTP, L2TP, SSTP and IKEv2, it can even work to connect devices such as smartphones and tablets to your network.

There is a third function available within the Server 2016 Remote Access role called the **Web Application Proxy** (**WAP**). This function is not used for connecting remote computers fully into the network such as is the case with DirectAccess and VPN; rather, WAP is used for publishing internal web resources out to the Internet. For example, if you are running Exchange and SharePoint Server inside your network and want to publish access to these web-based resources to the Internet for external users to connect to, WAP would be a mechanism that could publish access to these resources. The term for publishing to the Internet like this is Reverse Proxy, and WAP can act as such. It can also behave as an ADFS Proxy.

For further information on the WAP role, please visit `http://technet.microsoft.com/en-us/library/dn584107.aspx`.

DirectAccess planning question and answers

One of the most confusing parts about setting up DirectAccess is that there are many different ways to do it. Some are good ideas, while others are not. Before we get rolling with recipes, we are going to cover a series of questions and answers to help guide you towards a successful DA deployment. One of the first questions that always presents itself when setting up DirectAccess is *How do I assign IP addresses to my DA server?*. This is quite a loaded question because the answer depends on how you plan to implement DA, which features you plan to utilize, and even upon how secure you believe your DA server to be. Let me ask you some questions, pose potential answers to those questions, and discuss the effects of making each decision.

- Which client operating systems can connect using DirectAccess?

  Windows 7 Ultimate, Windows 7 Enterprise, Windows 8.x Enterprise, and Windows 10 Enterprise or Education. You'll notice that the Professional SKU is missing from this list. That is correct; Windows 7, Windows 8, and Windows 10 Pro do *not* contain the DirectAccess connectivity components. Yes, this does mean that Surface Pro tablets cannot utilize DirectAccess out-of-the-box. However, I have seen many companies now install Windows 10 Enterprise onto their Surface tablets, effectively turning them into *Surface Enterprises*. This works well and does indeed enable them to be DA clients. In fact, I am currently typing this text on a DirectAccess connected Surface *Pro turned Enterprise* tablet.

- Do I need one or two NICs on my DirectAccess server?

  Technically, you could set up either way. In practice, however, it really is designed for dual-NIC implementation. Single NIC DirectAccess works okay sometimes to establish a proof-of-concept to test out the technology, but I have seen too many problems with single NIC implementations in the field to ever recommend it for production use. Stick with two network cards, one facing the internal network and one facing the Internet.

- Do my DirectAccess servers have to be joined to the domain?

  Yes.

- Does DirectAccess have site-to-site failover capabilities?

  Yes, though only Windows 8.x and 10 client computers can take advantage of it. This functionality is called Multi-Site DirectAccess. Multiple DA servers that are spread out geographically can be joined together in a multi-site array. Windows 8 and 10 client computers keep track of each individual entry point and are able to swing between them as needed or at user preference. Windows 7 clients do not have this capability and will always connect through their primary site.

- What are these things called 6to4, Teredo, and IP-HTTPS that I have seen in the Microsoft documentation?

  6to4, Teredo, and IP-HTTPS are all IPv6 transition tunneling protocols. All DirectAccess packets that are moving across the Internet between a DA client and DA server are IPv6 packets. If your internal network is IPv4, then when those packets reach the DirectAccess server they get turned down into IPv4 packets by some special components called DNS64 and NAT64. While these functions handle the translation of packets from IPv6 into IPv4 when necessary inside the corporate network, the key point here is that all DirectAccess packets that are traveling over the Internet part of the connection are always IPv6. Since the majority of the Internet is still IPv4, this means that we must tunnel those IPv6 packets inside something to get them across the Internet. That is the job of 6to4, Teredo, and IP-HTTPS. 6to4 encapsulates IPv6 packets into IPv4 headers and shuttles them around the Internet using protocol 41. Teredo similarly encapsulates IPv6 packets inside IPv4 headers, but then uses UDP port 3544 to transport them. IP-HTTPS encapsulates IPv6 inside IPv4 and then inside HTTP encrypted with TLS, essentially creating an HTTPS stream across the Internet. This, like any HTTPS traffic, utilizes TCP port 443. The DirectAccess traffic traveling inside either kind of tunnel is always encrypted since DirectAccess itself is protected by IPsec.

- Do I want to enable my clients to connect using Teredo?

  Most of the time, the answer here is yes. Probably the biggest factor that weighs on this decision is whether or not you are still running Windows 7 clients. When Teredo is enabled in an environment, this gives the client computers an opportunity to connect using Teredo, rather than all clients connecting in over the IP-HTTPS protocol. IP-HTTPS is sort of the catch-all for connections (it is used whenever Teredo and 6to4 are unavailable), but Teredo will be preferred by clients if it is available. For Windows 7 clients, Teredo is quite a bit faster than IP-HTTPS. So enabling Teredo on the server side means your Windows 7 clients (the ones connecting via Teredo) will have quicker response times, and the load on your DirectAccess server will be lessened. This is because Windows 7 clients connecting over IP-HTTPS are encrypting all of the traffic twice. This also means that the DA server is encrypting/decrypting everything that comes and goes twice. In Windows 8 and 10, there is an enhancement that brings IP-HTTPS performance almost on a par with Teredo, and so environments that are fully upgraded to Windows 8 and higher will receive less benefit from the extra work that goes into making sure Teredo works.

- Can I place my DirectAccess server behind a NAT?

  Yes, though there is a downside. Teredo cannot work if the DirectAccess server is sitting behind a NAT. For Teredo to be available, the DA server must have an External NIC with two consecutive *public* IP addresses. True public addresses. If you place your DA server behind any kind of NAT, Teredo will not be available and all clients will connect using the IP-HTTPS protocol. Again, if you are using Windows 7 clients, this will decrease their speed and increase the load on your DirectAccess server.

- How many IP addresses do I need on a standalone DirectAccess server?

  I am going to leave single NIC implementation out of this answer since I don't recommend it anyway. For scenarios where you are sitting the External NIC behind a NAT or, for any other reason, are limiting your DA to IP-HTTPS only, then we need one external address and one internal address. The external address can be a true public address or a private NATed DMZ address. Same with the internal; it could be a true internal IP or a DMZ IP. Make sure both NICs are not plugged into the same DMZ, however. For a better installation scenario that allows Teredo connections to be possible, you would need two consecutive public IP addresses on the External NIC and a single internal IP on the Internal NIC. This internal IP could be either a true internal or DMZ, but the public IPs really have to be public for Teredo to work.

- Do I need an internal PKI?

  Maybe. If you want to connect Windows 7 clients, then the answer is yes. If you are completely Windows 8 and above, then technically you do not need an internal PKI. But you really should use it anyway. Using an internal PKI, which can be a single, simple Windows CA server, greatly increases the security of your DirectAccess infrastructure. You'll find out during this chapter just how easy it is to implement certificates as part of the tunnel building authentication process, making your connections stronger and more secure.

Configuring DirectAccess, VPN, or a combination of the two

Now that we have some general ideas about how we want to implement our remote access technologies, where do we begin? Most services that you want to run on a Windows Server begin with a role installation, but the implementation of remote access begins before that. Let's walk through the process of taking a new server and turning it into a Microsoft Remote Access server.

Getting ready

All of our work will be accomplished on a new Windows Server 2016. We are taking the two-NIC approach to networking, and so we have two NICs installed on this server. The Internal NIC is plugged into the corporate network and the External NIC is plugged into the Internet for the sake of simplicity. The External NIC could just as well be plugged into a DMZ.

How to do it...

Follow these steps to turn your new server into a Remote Access server:

1. Assign IP addresses to your server. Since this is a multi-homed system with both internal and external networks connected, make sure you follow the steps in the Multi-homing your Windows Server 2016 recipe in `Chapter 1`, *Security and Networking*. Remember, the most important part is making sure that the Default Gateway goes on the External NIC only.

2. Join the new server to your domain.

3. Install an SSL certificate onto your DirectAccess server, which you plan to use for the IP-HTTPS listener. This is typically a certificate purchased from a public CA. If you own a wildcard SSL certificate, that will work perfectly!

4. If you're planning to use client certificates for authentication, make sure to pull down a copy of the certificate from your internal CA to your DirectAccess server.

 You want to make sure certificates are in place before you start the configuration of DirectAccess. This way the wizards will be able to automatically pull in information about those certificates during the first run. If you don't, DA will set itself up to use self-signed certificates, which are a security no-no.

5. Use **Server Manager** to install the **Remote Access** role. You should only do this after completing the previous steps.

6. If you plan to load balance multiple DirectAccess servers together at a later time, make sure to also install the feature called **Network Load Balancing**.

7. After selecting your role and feature, you will be asked which Remote Access role services you want to install. For our purposes of getting the remote workforce connected back into the corporate network, we want to choose **DirectAccess and VPN (RAS)**:

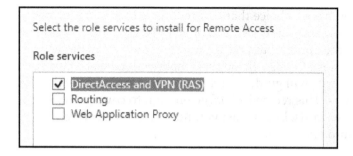

Select the role services to install for Remote Access

Role services

☑ DirectAccess and VPN (RAS)
☐ Routing
☐ Web Application Proxy

8. Now that the role has been successfully installed, you will see a yellow exclamation mark notification near the top of **Server Manager** indicating that you have some **Post-deployment Configuration** that needs to be done.

Do *not* click on **Open the Getting Started Wizard!**

9. Unfortunately, **Server Manager** leads you to believe that launching the **Getting Started Wizard (GSW)** is the logical next step. However, using the GSW as the mechanism for configuring your DirectAccess settings is kind of like roasting a marshmallow with a pair of tweezers. In order to ensure you have the full range of options available to you as you configure your remote access settings and that you don't get burned later, make sure to launch the configuration this way:

10. Click on the **Tools** menu from inside **Server Manager** and launch the **Remote Access Management Console**.

11. In the left window pane, navigate to **Configuration | DirectAccess and VPN**.

12. Click on the second link, the one that says **Run the Remote Access Setup Wizard**. Please note that once again the top option is to run that pesky Getting Started Wizard. Don't do it! I'll explain why in the *How it works...* section of this recipe:

➔ Run the Remote Access Setup Wizard

Use this wizard to configure DirectAccess and VPN with custom settings.

13. Now you have a choice that you will have to answer for yourself. Are you configuring only DirectAccess, only VPN, or a combination of the two? Simply click on the option that you want to deploy. Following your choice, you will see a series of steps (Steps 1 through 4) that need to be accomplished. This series of mini-wizards will guide you through the remainder of the DirectAccess and VPN particulars. This recipe isn't large enough to cover every specific option included in those wizards, but at least you now know the correct way to bring a DA/VPN server into operation.

How it works...

The remote access technologies included in Server 2016 have great functionality, but their initial configuration can be confusing. Following the procedure listed in this recipe will set you on the right path to be successful in your deployment, and prevent you from running into issues down the road. The reasons that I absolutely recommend you stay away from using the shortcut deployment method provided by the Getting Started Wizard are twofold:

- GSW skips a lot of options as it sets up DirectAccess, so you don't really have any understanding of how it works after finishing. You may have DA up-and-running, but have no idea how it's authenticating or working under the hood. This holds so much potential for problems later, should anything suddenly stop working.

- GSW employs a number of bad security practices in order to save time and effort in the setup process. For example, using the GSW usually means that your DirectAccess server will be authenticating users without client certificates, which is not a best practice. Also, it will co-host something called the NLS website on itself, which is also not a best practice. Those who utilize the GSW to configure DirectAccess will find that their GPO, which contains the client connectivity settings, will be security-filtered to the Domain Computers group. Even though it also contains a WMI filter that is supposed to limit that policy application to only mobile hardware like laptops, this is a terribly scary thing to see inside GPO filtering settings. You probably don't want all of your laptops to immediately start getting DA connectivity settings, but that is exactly what the GSW does for you. Perhaps worst, the GSW will create and make use of self-signed SSL certificates to validate its web traffic, even the traffic coming in from the Internet! This is a terrible practice and is the number one reason that should convince you that clicking on the Getting Started Wizard is not in your best interests.

Pre-staging Group Policy Objects to be used by DirectAccess

One of the great things about DirectAccess is that all of the connectivity settings the client computers need in order to connect are contained within a **Group Policy Objects** (**GPO**). This means that you can turn new client computers into DirectAccess-connected clients without ever touching that system. Once configured properly, all you need to do is add the new computer account to an Active Directory security group and, during the next automatic Group Policy refresh cycle (usually within 90 minutes), that new laptop will be connecting via DirectAccess whenever outside the corporate network.

You can certainly choose not to pre-stage anything with the GPOs and DirectAccess will still work. When you get to the end of the DA configuration wizard, it will inform you that two new GPOs are about to be created inside Active Directory. One GPO is used to contain the DirectAccess server settings, and the other GPO is used to contain the DirectAccess client settings. If you allow the wizard to handle the generation of these GPOs, it will create them, link them, filter them, and populate them with settings automatically. About half of the time, I see folks do it this way and are forever happy with letting the wizard manage those GPOs now and in the future.

The other half of the time, it is desired that we maintain a little more personal control over the GPOs. If you are setting up a new DA environment but your credentials don't have permission to create GPOs, the wizard is not going to be able to create them either. In this case, you will need to work with someone on your Active Directory team to get them created. Another reason to manage the GPOs manually is to have better control over placement of these policies. When you let the DA wizard create the GPOs, it will link them to the top level of your domain. It also sets Security Filtering on those GPOs so they are not going to be applied to everything in your domain, but when you open up the **Group Policy Management** console you will always see those DA policies listed right up there at the top level of the domain. Sometimes this is simply not desirable. So for this reason as well, you may want to choose to create and manage the GPOs by hand, so that we can secure placement and links where we specifically want them to be located.

Getting ready

While the DirectAccess wizards themselves are run from the DA server, our work with this recipe is not. The Group Policy settings that we will be configuring are all accomplished within Active Directory, and we will be doing the work from a Domain Controller in our environment.

How to do it...

To pre-stage GPOs for use with DirectAccess, follow these steps:

1. In your Domain Controller, launch the **Group Policy Management Console**.
2. Navigate to **Forest | Domains | Your Domain Name**. There should be a listing here called **Group Policy Objects**. Right-click on that and choose **New**.
3. Name your new GPO something like `DirectAccess Server Settings`.
4. Click on the new **DirectAccess Server Settings** GPO and it should open up automatically to the **Scope** tab. We need to adjust the **Security Filtering** section so that this GPO only applies to our DirectAccess server. This is a critical step for each GPO to ensure the settings that are going to be placed here do not get applied to the wrong computers.
5. Remove **Authenticated Users** that are prepopulated in that list. The list should now be empty.
6. Click the **Add...** button and search for the computer account of your DirectAccess server. Mine is called `RA1`. By default, this window will only search user accounts, so you will need to adjust **Object Types** to include **Computers** before it will allow you to add your server to this filtering list.
7. Your **Security Filtering** list should now look like this:

8. Now click on the **Details** tab of your GPO.
9. Change the **GPO Status** to **User configuration settings disabled**. We do this because our GPO is only going to contain computer-level settings, nothing at the user level.
10. The last thing to do is link your GPO to an appropriate container. Since we have Security Filtering enabled, our GPO is only ever going to apply its settings to the RA1 server but, without creating a link, the GPO will not even attempt to apply itself to anything. My RA1 server is sitting inside the OU called **Remote Access Servers**, so I will right-click on my **Remote Access Servers** OU and choose **Link an Existing GPO...**:

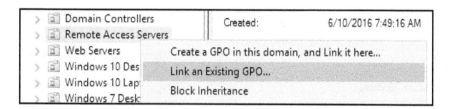

11. Choose the new **DirectAccess Server Settings** from the list of available GPOs and click on the **OK** button. This creates the link and puts the GPO into action. Since there are not yet any settings inside the GPO, it won't actually make any changes on the server. The DA configuration wizards take care of populating the GPO with the settings that are needed.

12. Now we simply need to rinse and repeat all of these steps to create another GPO, something like **DirectAccess Client Settings**. You want to set up the client settings GPO in the same way. Make sure that it is filtering to only the Active Directory Security Group that you created to contain your DirectAccess client computers. And make sure to link it to an appropriate container that will include those computer accounts. So maybe your client's GPO will look something like this:

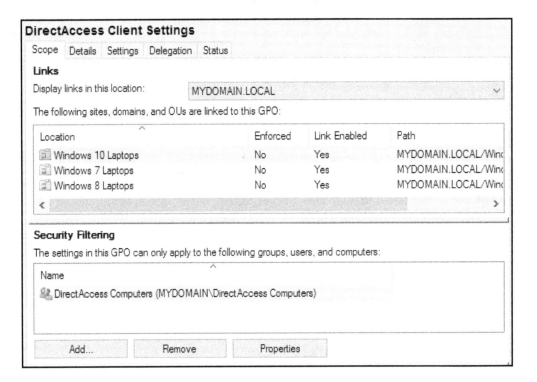

How it works...

Creating GPOs in Active Directory is a simple enough task, but it is critical that you configure the Links and Security Filtering correctly. If you do not take care to ensure that these DirectAccess connection settings are only going to apply to the machines that actually need the settings, you could create a world of trouble with internal servers getting remote access connection settings and causing them issues with connection while inside the network.

The key factors here are to make sure your DirectAccess Server Settings GPO applies to only the DA server or servers in your environment, and that the DirectAccess Client Settings GPO applies to only the DA client computers that you plan to enable in your network. The best practice here is to specify this GPO to only apply to a specific Active Directory security group so that you have full control over which computer accounts are in that group. I have seen some folks do it based only on the OU links and include whole OUs in the filtering for the clients GPO (foregoing the use of an AD group at all), but doing it this way makes it quite a bit more difficult to add or remove machines from the access list in the future.

Enhancing the security of DirectAccess by requiring certificate authentication

When a DirectAccess client computer builds its IPsec tunnels back to the corporate network, it has the ability to require a certificate as part of that authentication process. In earlier versions of DirectAccess, the one in Server 2008 R2 and the one provided by **Unified Access Gateway** (**UAG**), these certificates were required in order to make DirectAccess work. Setting up the certificates really isn't a big deal at all. As long as there is a CA server in your network, you are already prepared to issue the necessary certificates at no cost. Unfortunately, though, there must have been enough complaints back to Microsoft in order for them to make these certificates recommended instead of required, and they created a new mechanism in Windows 8 and Server 2012 called Kerberos proxy that can be used to authenticate the tunnels instead. This allows the DirectAccess tunnels to build without the computer certificate, making that authentication process easier to set up initially, but less secure overall.

I'm here to strongly recommend that you still utilize certificates in your installs! They are not difficult to set up, and using them makes your tunnel authentication stronger. Further, many of you may not have a choice and will still be required to install these certificates. Only simple DirectAccess scenarios that are all Windows 8 or higher on the client side can get away with the shortcut method of foregoing certificates. Anybody who still wants to connect Windows 7 via DirectAccess will need to use certificates as part of their implementation. In addition to Windows 7 access, anyone who intends to use the advanced features of DirectAccess, such as load balancing, multi-site, or two-factor authentication, will also need to utilize these certificates. With any of these scenarios, certificates become a requirement again, not a recommendation.

In my experience, almost everyone still has Windows 7 clients that would benefit from being DirectAccess-connected, and it's always a good idea to make your DA environment redundant by having load-balanced servers. This further emphasizes the point that you should just set up certificate authentication right out of the gate, whether or not you need it initially. You might decide to make a change later that would require certificates, and it would be easier to have them installed from the get-go than trying to incorporate them later into a running DA environment.

Getting ready

In order to distribute certificates, you will need a CA server running in your network. Once certificates are distributed to the appropriate places, the rest of our work will be accomplished from our Server 2016 DirectAccess server.

How to do it...

Follow these steps to make use of certificates as part of the DirectAccess tunnel authentication process:

1. The first thing that you need to do is distribute certificates to your DA servers and all DA client computers. The easiest way to do this is by building a new template on the CA server that is duplicated from the in-built Computer template. Whenever I create a custom template for use with DirectAccess, I try to make sure that it meets the following criteria:
   - The **Subject Name** of the certificate should match the **Common Name** of the computer (which is also the FQDN of the computer)
   - The **Subject Alternative Name (SAN)** of the certificate should match the **DNS Name** of the computer (which is also the FQDN of the computer)
   - The certificate should serve the **Intended Purposes** of both **Client Authentication** and **Server Authentication**

2. For the actual distribution of these certificates, I'm going to direct you to review a couple of other recipes in this book. You can issue these certificates manually using Microsoft Management Console (MMC), as described in the Using MMC to request a new certificate recipe in Chapter 2, *Working with Certificates*. Otherwise, you can lessen your hands-on administrative duties by enabling Autoenrollment, discussed in the Configuring Autoenrollment to issue certificates to all domain joined systems recipe in Chapter 2, *Working with Certificates*.

3. Now that we have certificates distributed to our DirectAccess clients and servers, log-in to your primary DirectAccess server and open up the **Remote Access Management Console**.

4. Click on **Configuration** in the top-left corner. You should now see steps 1 through 4 listed.

5. Click **Edit...** listed under **Step 2**.

6. Now you can either click **Next** twice or click on the word **Authentication** to jump directly to the authentication screen.

7. Check the box that says **Use computer certificates**.

8. Now we have to specify the Certification Authority server that issued our client certificates. If you used an intermediary CA to issue your certificates, make sure to check the appropriate checkbox. Otherwise, most of the time, certificates are issued from a root CA, and in this case, you would simply click on the **Browse...** button and look for your CA in the list:

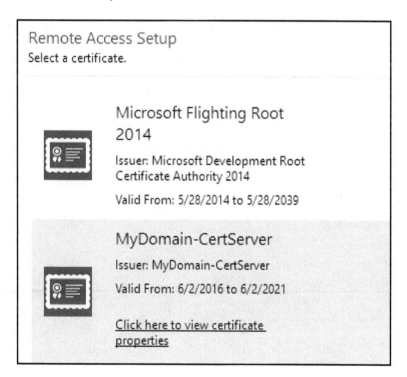

This screen is sometimes confusing because people expect to have to choose the certificate itself from the list. This is not the case. What you are actually choosing from this list is the CA server that issued the certificates.

9. Make any other appropriate selections on the **Authentication** screen. For example, many times when we require client certificates for authentication, it is because we have Windows 7 computers that we want to connect via DirectAccess. If that is the case for you, select the checkbox for **Enable Windows 7 client computers to connect via DirectAccess**:

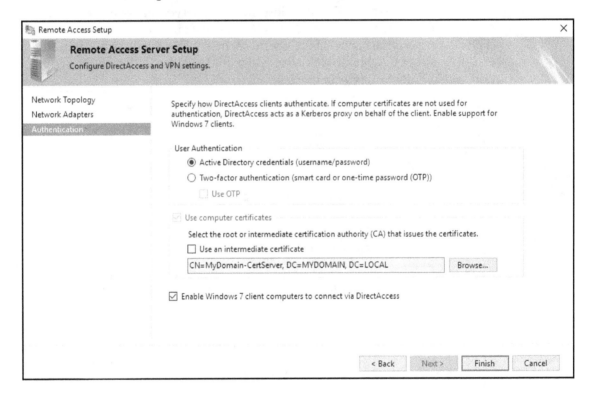

How it works...

Requiring certificates as part of your DirectAccess tunnel authentication process is a good idea in any environment. It makes the solution more secure and enables advanced functionality. The primary driver for most companies to require these certificates is the enablement of Windows 7 clients to connect via DirectAccess, but I suggest that anyone using DirectAccess in any capacity make use of these certs. They are simple to deploy, easy to configure and give you some extra peace of mind knowing that only computers with a certificate issued directly to them from your own internal CA server are going to be able to connect through your DirectAccess entry point.

Building your Network Location Server on its own system

If you zipped through the default settings when configuring DirectAccess, or worse, used the Getting Started Wizard, chances are that your **Network Location Server** (**NLS**) is running right on the DirectAccess server itself. This is not the recommended method for using NLS; it really should be running on a separate web server. In fact, if you want to do something more advanced later, such as setting up load-balanced DirectAccess servers, you're going to have to move NLS onto a different server anyway, so you might as well do it right the first time.

NLS is a very simple requirement, but a critical one. It is just a website, it doesn't matter what content the site has, and it only has to run inside your network. Nothing has to be externally available. In fact, nothing should be externally available, because you only want this site accessed internally. This NLS website is a large part of the mechanism by which DirectAccess client computers figure out when they are inside the office and when they are outside. If they can see the NLS website, they know they are inside the network and will disable DirectAccess name resolution, effectively turning off DA. If they do not see the NLS website, they will assume they are outside the corporate network and enable DirectAccess name resolution.

There are two *gotchas* with setting up an NLS website:

- The first is that it must be HTTPS, so it does need a valid SSL certificate. Since this website is only running inside the network and being accessed from domain-joined computers, this SSL certificate can easily be one that has been issued from your internal CA server. So there's no cost associated there.
- The second catch that I have encountered a number of times is that for some reason the default IIS splash screen page doesn't make for a very good NLS website. If you set up a standard IIS web server and use the default site as NLS, sometimes it works to validate the connections and sometimes it doesn't. Given that, I always set up a specific site that I create myself, just to be on the safe side.

So let's work together to follow the exact process I always take when setting up NLS websites in a new DirectAccess environment.

Getting ready

Our NLS website will be hosted on an IIS server that runs Server 2016. Most of the work will be accomplished from this web server, but we will also be creating a DNS record and will utilize a Domain Controller for that task.

How to do it...

Let's work together to set up our new Network Location Server website:

1. First, decide on an internal DNS name to use for this website and set it up in DNS of your domain. I am going to use `nls.mydomain.local` and am creating a regular Host (A) record, which points `nls.mydomain.local` to the IP address of my web server.
2. Now log in to that web server and let's create some simple content for this new website. Create a new folder called `C:\NLS`.
3. Inside your new folder, create a new `Default.htm` file.
4. Edit this file and throw some simple text in there. I usually say something like `This is the NLS website used by DirectAccess. Please do not delete or modify me!`:

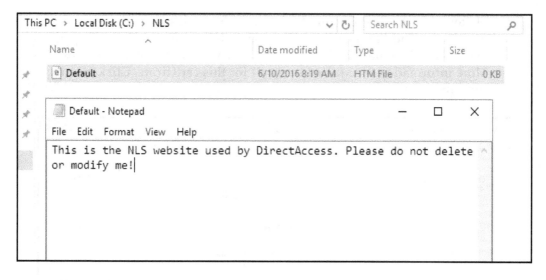

5. Remember, this needs to be an HTTPS website, so before we try setting up the actual website, we should acquire the SSL certificate that we need to use with this site. Since this certificate is coming from my internal CA server, I'm going to open up MMC on my web server to accomplish this task.

6. Once MMC is opened, snap in the **Certificates** module. Make sure to choose **Computer account** and then **Local computer** when it prompts you for which certificate store you want to open.

7. Navigate to **Certificates (Local Computer) | Personal | Certificates**.

8. Right-click on this **Certificates** folder and choose **All Tasks | Request New Certificate...**

9. Click **Next** twice and you should see your list of certificate templates that are available on your internal CA server. If you do not see one that looks appropriate for requesting a website certificate, you may need to check over the settings on your CA server to make sure the correct templates are configured for issuance.

10. My template is called **Custom Web Server**. Since this is a web server certificate, there is some additional information that I need to provide in my request in order to successfully issue a certificate. So I go ahead and click on the link that says **More information is required to enroll for this certificate. Click here to configure settings**:

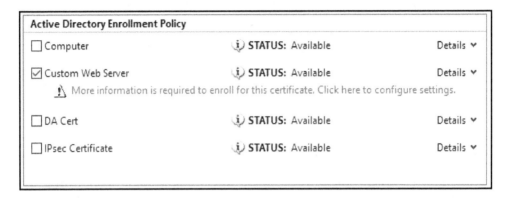

11. Drop down the **Subject name | Type** menu and choose the **Common name** option.
12. Enter a common name for our website into the **Value** field, which in my case is `nls.mydomain.local.`
13. Click the **Add** button, and your CN should move over to the right side of the screen like this:

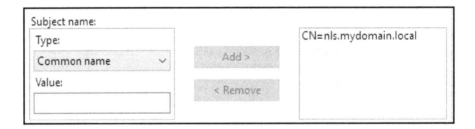

14. Click on **OK** then click on the **Enroll** button. You should now have an SSL certificate sitting in your certificates store that can be used to authenticate traffic moving to our `nls.mydomain.local` name.
15. Open up **Internet Information Services (IIS) Manager** and browse to the **Sites** folder. Go ahead and remove the default website that IIS had automatically set up so that we can create our own NLS website without any fear of conflict.

16. Click on the **Add Website...** button.
17. Populate the information as shown in the following screenshot. Make sure to choose your own IP address and SSL certificate from the lists, of course:

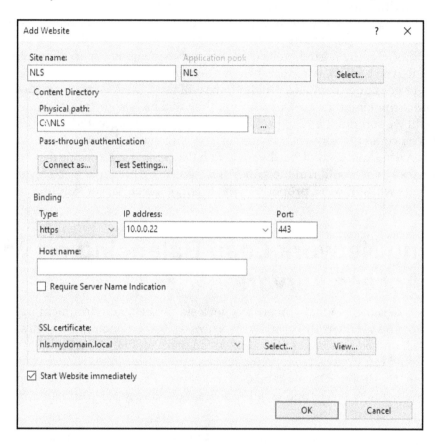

18. Click the **OK** button, and you now have an NLS website running successfully in your network. You should be able to open up a browser on a client computer sitting inside the network and successfully browse to `https://nls.mydomain.local`.

How it works...

In this recipe, we configured a basic Network Location Server website for use with our DirectAccess environment. This site will do exactly what we need it to when our DA client computers try to validate whether they are inside or outside the corporate network. While this recipe meets our requirements for NLS, and in fact puts us into the good practice of installing with NLS being hosted on its own web server, there is yet another step you could take to make it even better. Currently, this web server is a single point of failure for NLS. If this web server goes down or has a problem, we will have DirectAccess client computers inside the office thinking they are outside, and they will have some major name resolution problems until we sort out the NLS problem. Given that, it is a great idea to make NLS redundant. You could cluster servers together, use **Microsoft Network Load Balancing (NLB)**, or even use some kind of hardware load balancer if you have one available in your network. This way you could run the same NLS website on multiple web servers and know that your clients will still work properly in the event of a web server failure.

Enabling Network Load Balancing on your DirectAccess servers

DirectAccess is designed so that you always get a single server environment up-and-running first before you start tinkering with arrays or load balancing. This way you can validate that all of the environmental factors are in place and working and that you can successfully build DA tunnels from your client computers before introducing any further complexity into the design. Once established, however, it is a common next step to look into turning up another new server and creating some redundancy for your new remote access solution.

While joining two similar servers together to share the load is commonly called clustering, and sometimes I hear admins refer to it as such in the DirectAccess world, load balancing DA servers together actually has nothing to do with Windows Clustering. When you install both the remote access role and the Network Load Balancing feature onto your remote access servers, you have already equipped them with all the parts and pieces they need in order to communicate with each other and run an Active/Active sharing configuration. The operating system will make use of Windows NLB to shuttle traffic to the appropriate destinations, but everything inside NLB gets configured from the **Remote Access Management** Console. This gives you a nice visual console that can be used to administer and manage those NLB settings right alongside your other remote access settings.

Once DirectAccess is established and running on a single server, there really are just a couple of quick wizards to run through to configure this NLB. However, the verbiage in these options can be quite confusing, especially if you're not overly familiar with the way that DirectAccess transmits packets. So let's take some time to walk through creating an array from our existing DA server and adding a second node to that array.

Getting ready

We are going to use our existing RA1 server, which is already running DirectAccess. This and our new server, RA2, are both running Windows Server 2016. They both have the Remote Access role and the Network Load Balancing feature installed. Both are joined to our domain and have their required certificates (SSL and IPsec) installed for use with DirectAccess. The same SSL certificate has been installed to both servers; since they are going to be sharing the load and all requests to both systems will be coming in from the same public DNS name, they are able to share that certificate.

If your DirectAccess servers are virtual machines, there is one very important prerequisite. You must go into your VM's NIC settings and choose the **Enable spoofing of MAC addresses** option. Without this box checked for each of the NICs, your network traffic will stop working altogether when you create a load balanced array.

How to do it...

For the purposes of this recipe, we are going to assume that RA1 has been configured for use with Teredo, meaning that it has two public IP addresses assigned on the External NIC. We are using this as an example because it is the most complex configuration to walk through when setting up NLB. The same procedure applies for a single IP on the External NIC; it would simply mean that you are only configuring one **virtual IP** (**VIP**) instead of two.

1. First, we need to have a clear understanding of which IP addresses are going to be used where. This is critical information to possess and understand before trying to start any kind of configuration. The current RA1 IP addresses are as follows:
   - **External IPs**: 1.1.1.10 and 1.1.1.11
   - **Internal IP**: 10.0.0.7

2. These three IP addresses that are currently running on RA1 are going to turn into our **virtual IPs** (**VIPs**). These are the IP addresses that are going to be shared between both DirectAccess servers. Since we are changing the roles of these IPs, this means that we need to dedicate new **dedicated IPs** (**DIPs**), both internally and externally, to both RA1 and RA2.

3. New IP address assignments are shown as follows:
   - **External VIPs (shared)**: 1.1.1.10 and 1.1.1.11
   - **Internal VIP (shared)**: 10.0.0.7
   - **RA1 External DIP**: 1.1.1.12
   - **RA1 Internal DIP**: 10.0.0.8
   - **RA2 External DIP**: 1.1.1.13
   - **RA2 Internal DIP**: 10.0.0.9

4. So, to summarize, when using Teredo (dual public IPs) and creating a two-node DirectAccess server load balanced array, you will need a total of four public IP addresses and three internal IP addresses.

5. On RA1, we are going to leave the VIPs in place for now. The DirectAccess wizards will change them for us later.

6. On the new RA2 server, set its final DIP addresses on the NICs. So in our example, the External NIC gets 1.1.1.13 and the Internal NIC gets 10.0.0.9.

7. There are only four steps to take on a DirectAccess array node server such as RA2, or any additional DA server that you want to add to the array in the future:
   - Assign IP addresses.
   - Join it to the domain.
   - Install the certificates.
   - Add the Remote Access role and Network Load Balancing feature.

8. The remainder of its configuration is accomplished from the Remote Access Management Console on RA1.

9. On RA1, your primary DirectAccess server, open **Remote Access Management Console**.

10. In the left window pane, navigate to **Configuration | DirectAccess and VPN**.

11. Now, over in the right-hand **Tasks** pane, down at the bottom, choose **Enable Load Balancing**:

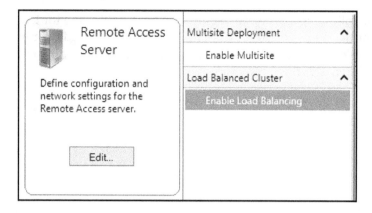

12. Click **Next**.

13. Choose **Use Windows Network Load Balancing (NLB)**. You can see there is also an option for using an external load balancer, if you have one available to you. I find that the majority of customers utilize the built-in NLB, even when hardware load balancers are available.

14. The next screen is **External Dedicated IP Addresses**. This is where things start to get confusing and mistakes are often made. If you read the text on this screen, it is telling you that the current IP addresses assigned to the NICs are now going to be used as VIPs. You do not need to specify anything about the VIPs on this screen. Instead, what we are doing on this screen and the next is specifying what *new* DIPs are now going to be assigned to the physical NICs on this server. First, since this is the external screen, we specify our new public IP that will be used by RA1:

15. On the following screen, do the same thing but this time for the Internal NIC. The current IP address of 10.0.0.7 is going to be converted over into a shared VIP, and so we need to specify the new Internal DIP that is going to be assigned to RA1's Internal NIC.

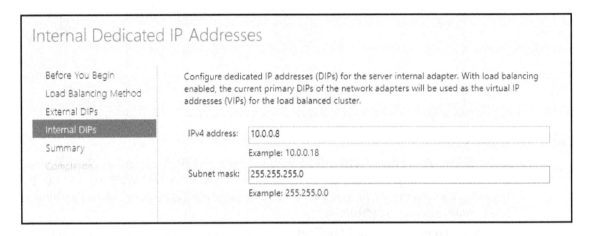

Now you can see why having a definitive list of IP addresses before starting this wizard is important!

16. Click **Next**, then if everything looks correct in the **Summary** screen, go ahead and click on the **Commit** button. This will roll the changes into the GPO settings and apply the changes to our RA1 server. Remember, nothing has been done to RA2 yet as we haven't specified anything about it in these screens. We now have an active array, but so far there is only one member, RA1.

17. Now that you are back inside the main **Configuration** screen, go ahead and navigate to **Load Balanced Cluster** | **Add or Remove Servers**:

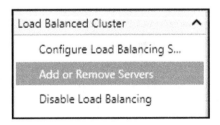

18. Click on the **Add Server...** button.

19. Input the FQDN of your second server. Mine is RA2.MYDOMAIN.LOCAL. Then click **Next**.

20. If you have appropriately configured your second **Remote Access Server** with correct IP address information and the certificates that it needs, the **Network Adapters** screen should self-populate all of the necessary information. Double-check this info to make sure it looks correct and click **Next**:

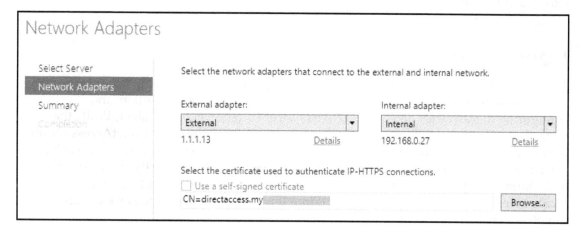

21. If the **Summary** page all looks correct, click on the **Add** button.

22. Click **Close**. Then back in the **Add or Remove Servers** screen, you should now see both of your Remote Access Servers in the list. Go ahead and click on the **Commit** button to finalize the addition of this second node:

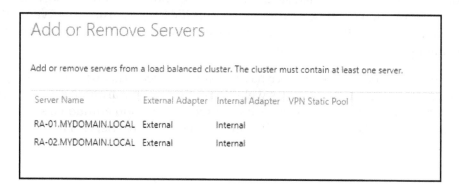

Following the addition of the second node, I always go back into the NIC properties of both NICs on both servers and make sure that all of the expected IP addresses got added correctly. Sometimes I find that the wizard is not able to successfully populate all of the VIPs and DIPs, and that I have to add them manually afterwards. Each NIC now has a specific DIP, as listed at the beginning of this recipe. In addition to those DIPs, the External NIC on each server should also list both External VIPs, and the Internal NIC on each server should list the Internal VIP. The TCP/IPv4 properties of the NICs sure look to be overly-populated with IP addresses, but this is all normal and well for a successfully load-balanced DirectAccess array.

How it works...

The ability to load balance DA servers together right out of the box with Windows Server 2016 is an incredibly nice feature. Redundancy is key for any good solution, and configuring this array for an Active/Active failover situation is a no-brainer. While the wizards for enabling NLB are centralized right alongside all the other DirectAccess settings, they can certainly be confusing when running through them for the first time. As with any system whose job is to shuttle network traffic around, planning correctly for IP addressing and routing is key to the success of your DirectAccess NLB deployment. Hopefully, this recipe helps to clear up questions surrounding this commonly requested task on our remote access servers.

Following the creation of your array, you will notice that navigation through some of the screens inside the **Remote Access Management** Console has changed slightly. When you access screens such as **Configuration** to make changes, **Operations Status** to check on the status of your servers, or **Remote Client Status** to see what clients are connected, you will now notice that the nodes are listed separately. You can now click on the individual node name to see information on those screens that is specific to one particular server in the array, or you can click on the words **Load Balanced Cluster** in order to see information that is shared among all of the array members.

One other important note. Now that we have a load balanced array up-and-running, it is easy to add a third node to this array as well! Your DirectAccess array can grow as your company grows, up to eight node servers if required. Simply add additional servers to this array by navigating to **Load Balanced Cluster** | **Add or Remove Servers task**.

Adding VPN to your existing DirectAccess server

It is fairly common when starting work with the new remote access role for administrators to choose the **Deploy DirectAccess only** option. Maybe you initially thought this box was only going to be used for DA, or that all of your client connections would be handled by only the DA role. While this is true for some organizations, it is pretty common to get some benefit from having both DirectAccess and VPN configured on your remote access entry point. Maybe you have some mobile phones or personal tablets that you want connected to the corporate network. Or perhaps you want to give the ability for home computers, or even Macs, to connect remotely. Another reason that enterprises are looking to enable VPN on their DirectAccess servers is to start testing or playing around with Always On VPN. These are scenarios that are outside the scope of DirectAccess and require some other form of VPN connectivity.

Making significant changes on a production server can be intimidating, and you want to make sure that you select the right options. Also, IP addressing remote access servers isn't always a cakewalk, and so it would be natural to assume that turning a DirectAccess server into a DirectAccess plus VPN server would involve some additional IP addressing. You would actually be wrong about that last one. VPN can share the public IP address already configured and running for your DA clients, so thankfully when you decide to add VPN to your server, you don't have to reconfigure the NICs in any way. Since we don't have to make networking changes first, let's jump right into taking our production DA server and adding the VPN role to it.

Getting ready

We are working today from our new DirectAccess server, which is a Windows Server 2016 that has the Remote Access role installed.

How to do it...

To add VPN functionality to your existing 2016 DirectAccess server, follow these steps:

1. Open **Remote Access Management Console** from the **Tools** menu inside **Server Manager**.

2. In the left window pane, navigate to **Configuration | DirectAccess and VPN**. This is the screen where you see the four setup steps listed in the middle.

3. Now over on the right, you see a section of buttons related to **VPN**. Go ahead and click on **Enable VPN**:

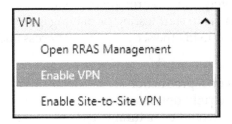

4. You will receive a pop-up message asking you to make sure you intend to configure VPN settings on this server. Go ahead and click **OK**. This will cause your remote access server to spin through some processes, reaching out to the GPOs and reconfiguring the necessary settings so that they include VPN connectivity.

5. VPN is now enabled on our server, but we have yet to configure IP addressing that will be handed out to the client computers. Once you are back at the main **Configuration** screen, click the `Edit...` button listed under **Step 2**.

6. There is now a fourth screen available inside this mini-wizard called **VPN Configuration**. Go ahead and click on that.

7. If you want VPN clients to pull IP addresses from an internal DHCP server, leave the radio button set to the top option. If you would rather specify a particular range of IP addresses that should be handed out to client computers, choose **Assign addresses from a static address pool** and specify the range of addresses in the given fields:

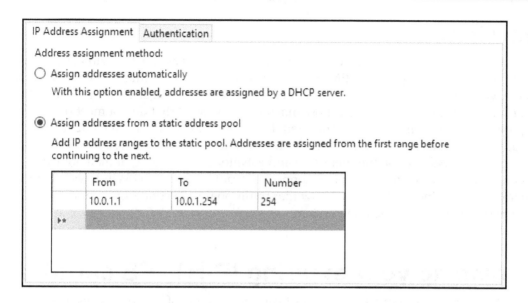

When you specify a static range like this, your remote access server will start handing out these addresses to the client computers that connect using VPN. However, these client computers will most likely not be able to connect to any internal resources without a little additional networking consideration. When you create a static address pool for assigning IP addresses to VPN clients, there are two rules you need to keep in mind:

- The pool of addresses to be handed out to clients should come from a subnet that does not exist in the remote access server's internal routing table. For example, my network is 10.0.0.x and I am going to assign VPN client licenses from 10.0.1.x.
- You need to set the default route for this other subnet so that it points back to the internal IP address of the remote access server. Without doing this, traffic from the VPN clients might make its way into the 10.0.1.x subnet, but responses from that subnet aren't going to know how to get back to the VPN client computers. By setting a default route on the 10.0.1.x subnet to point back to the Internal NIC of the remote access server, you fix this.

How it works...

The act of enabling VPN on a DirectAccess server is a single action, but without a couple of extra configuration steps, that VPN enablement isn't going to do much for you. With this recipe, you should now have the information you need to enable and configure a VPN on your remote access server and get those machines connected that do not meet the requirements to be DirectAccess-connected. In the field, I find that most companies try to get all the computers they can connected via DirectAccess, because it is a much easier technology to deal with on the client side and is better for managing domain joined systems. When faced with the need to connect computers that aren't Windows 7, 8, or 10, or are not domain joined, it is nice to know that traditional VPN connectivity options exist right in our Server 2016 operating system.

Replacing your expiring IP-HTTPS certificate

DirectAccess has the ability to utilize certificates in a couple of different ways. Depending on how you configure DA, there are different places that certificates may or may not be used, but one common variable in all DirectAccess implementations is **IP-HTTPS**. This is a transition technology that is always enabled on a DA server, and it requires an SSL certificate to work properly. IP-HTTPS traffic comes in from the Internet, and so I always recommend that the SSL certificate used for the IP-HTTPS listener should be one purchased from a public CA entity.

As with any SSL certificate, they are only valid for a certain time period. Typically, these certificates are purchased on a one-, two-, or three-year basis. This means that eventually, you will have to renew that certificate and figure out how to make DirectAccess recognize and utilize the new one. IP-HTTPS makes use of a web listener inside IIS, and so it is a natural assumption that, when you need to change your certificate, you do so inside IIS. This is an incorrect assumption. What's worse is that you can actually dig into the site inside IIS and change the certificate binding, and cause it to work for a while. This is not the correct place to change the certificate! If you simply change the binding inside IIS, your change will eventually be reversed and it will go back to using the old certificate. Unfortunately, I get calls quite regularly from customers who do this and then have all sorts of users unable to connect remotely because the DA server has reverted to using the old, now expired, certificate.

Let's work through this recipe together to configure our DirectAccess to utilize a new certificate that was recently purchased and installed onto our server.

Getting ready

We have DirectAccess up-and-running on our Windows Server 2016 Remote Access server. Our SSL certificate that we use for IP-HTTPS is about to expire and we have renewed it with our CA. The new copy of the certificate has already been downloaded and installed onto the server itself, so now we just need to figure out where it needs to be adjusted for DirectAccess to start using it.

How to do it...

To adjust the DirectAccess configuration to start using a new certificate for the IP-HTTPS listener, follow these steps:

1. Open **Remote Access Management Console** on your DirectAccess server.
2. In the left window pane, browse to **Configuration** | **DirectAccess and VPN**.
3. Under **Step 2** of the configuration, click on **Edit...**:

4. Click **Next**.

5. You will now see the currently assigned certificate for IP-HTTPS. This is the certificate that is about to expire. Go ahead and click on the **Browse...** button:

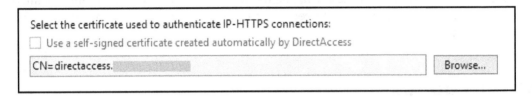

6. Now simply choose the new certificate with the new expiration date from the newly opened list of available certificates.

7. Click **Next** a couple more times to finish up the **Step 2** wizard.

 Keep in mind that the IP-HTTPS certificate is a per-node setting. If you have an array of multiple DirectAccess servers, you make all changes from the primary server's console, but you must install the certificate on each server and then make the certificate change on each node separately within the configuration.

8. At this point, nothing has actually been changed with the live configuration. To make this change active, you need to press the **Finish...** button, which is near the bottom of **Remote Access Management Console**:

9. If everything in the review looks good, click on **Apply**, and this will push your changes into action. The new certificate is now in place and working to validate those IP-HTTPS connections.

How it works...

Replacing the SSL certificate that is used by IP-HTTPS is a regular and necessary task for any DirectAccess server administrator, but one that only comes maybe once per year. This generally means that, by the time your certificate expiration date rolls around, you have probably forgotten where this setting is in the configuration. I hope this recipe can be a quick reference to alleviate that worry.

I always check the certificate from outside the network after making the change to ensure the new certificate is really the one that is now live on the system. If you take a computer outside of your network on the Internet, try browsing to a dummy site from your public DNS record on your DirectAccess server. For example, if the public DNS record that you are using on your server is `directaccess.contoso.com`, try browsing to `https://directaccess.contoso.com/test`. You can expect to get a 404 error because the page we are requesting doesn't actually exist, but when you get the 404 error you have the ability (depending on what browser you are using; I tend to prefer Chrome for this task) to view which certificate is being used to validate your web traffic. Click to view the certificate details and make sure that it is your new certificate with the newest validity dates. Further, if you encounter any kind of certificate warning message when you are trying to browse to this test website, this probably indicates that there is some kind of problem with the certificate and you may need to investigate it further.

Reporting on DirectAccess and VPN connections

One of the big benefits that Microsoft brought to the table in these newer versions of the remote access role is reporting. In the past, it was difficult to tell who was connected and even harder to find out what they were doing or when they had been connected previously. Historical reporting on remote sessions was kind of absent. All of that changes in the newer editions, as we now have a nice interface to show us who is connecting, how often they are connecting, and even some information on what things they are doing while they are connected. Here, we'll take a look into those interfaces and explore some of the information that is available to consume. We will also make sure you know how to turn on the historical reporting, as it is not enabled by default.

Getting ready

All work with this recipe will be accomplished from our Windows Server 2016 Remote Access server that is servicing both DirectAccess and VPN clients.

How to do it...

Follow these steps to get familiar with the remote access reporting options available in Server 2016:

1. Open **Remote Access Management Console** from the **Tools** menu inside **Server Manager**.
2. In the left window pane, browse to **Remote Client Status**. Here, you will see a list of all currently connected devices and users. This shows both DirectAccess connections and VPN connections.
3. If you click on a particular connection, you will see some additional data displayed below. You can easily find out whether the user is connected using DirectAccess or VPN, and some more specific information about their connection:

4. Look over toward the left a little where is says **Access Details** and you can even see what internal resources have been accessed by the user and computer.

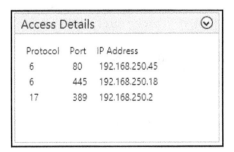

5. Once your environment is large enough that this screen becomes filled with connections, the **Search** box at the top comes in very handy. You simply type in any information you want to search for, and the results in the window will filter down to your search criteria.

6. If you would like to display more data on the screen, you can right-click on any of the existing column names and select additional columns to show or hide:

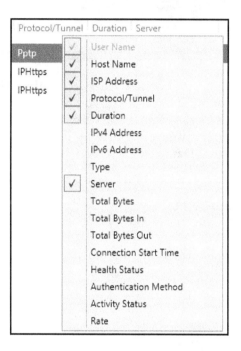

7. All of this information is great! But what if we want to look back and view this data historically? Maybe you want to view connections from the past day, or week. Maybe you need to come up with some kind of report on how many connections happened over the past month. In the left window pane, click on **Reporting** to get started with that.

8. Since reporting is not enabled by default, we don't have any data here yet. Instead, you will see a message indicating that you need to configure accounting. Go ahead and click on this link:

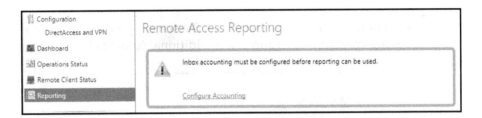

9. Now you have options for **Use RADIUS accounting**, **Use inbox accounting**, or both. RADIUS accounting implies that you have a RADIUS server set up and ready to accept this kind of data. I don't see many customers using this option. Instead, most select **Use inbox accounting**, which writes all of the data right to the **Windows Internal Database (WID)** on the DirectAccess server itself:

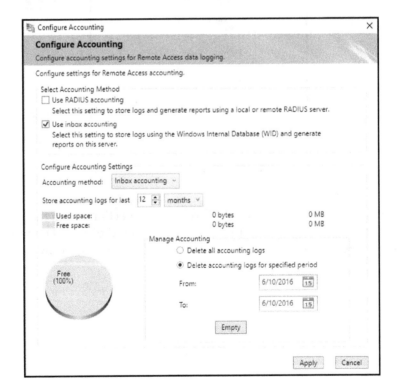

10. Once you have made your selection, click **Apply**. You will see that the **Reporting** screen now looks a lot more like the **Remote Client Status** screen, except that inside **Reporting**, you have additional options to select date ranges and pull historical information.

How it works...

The reporting of user connection data is critical to most remote access systems. The inclusion of this data, particularly for historical connections, is a great feature addition that I am sure every remote access administrator is going to make use of. With a simple configuration change, we set up our Windows Remote Access server to keep track of these DirectAccess and VPN connections so that we can run and save reports on that data in the future.

Other Books You May Enjoy

If you enjoyed this book, you may be interested in these other books by Packt:

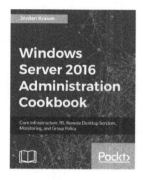

Windows Server 2016 Administration Cookbook

Jordan Krause

ISBN: 978-1-78913-593-0

- Become skilled in the navigation of Windows Server 2016, and explore the technologies and options that it provides
- Build the infrastructure required for a successful Windows Server network
- Move away from those open-source web server platforms and start migrating your websites to Server 2016's Internet Information Services today
- Provide a centralized point for users to access applications and data by confguring Remote Desktop Services
- Compose optimal Group Policies

Windows Server 2016 Automation with PowerShell Cookbook - Second Edition

Thomas Lee

ISBN: 978-1-78712-204-8

- Streamline routine administration processes
- Improve the performance and storage of your Windows server with enhanced large-scale PowerShell scripts
- Use DSC to leverage Windows server features
- Generate automatic reports that highlight unexpected changes in your environment
- Monitor performance and report on system utilization using detailed graphs and analysis
- Create and manage a reliable and redundant Hyper-V environment
- Manage your enterprise's patch level
- Utilize multiple tools and protocols to manage your environment

Leave a review - let other readers know what you think

Please share your thoughts on this book with others by leaving a review on the site that you bought it from. If you purchased the book from Amazon, please leave us an honest review on this book's Amazon page. This is vital so that other potential readers can see and use your unbiased opinion to make purchasing decisions, we can understand what our customers think about our products, and our authors can see your feedback on the title that they have worked with Packt to create. It will only take a few minutes of your time, but is valuable to other potential customers, our authors, and Packt. Thank you!

Index

www.ingramcontent.com/pod-product-compliance
Lightning Source LLC
Chambersburg PA
CBHW080536060326
40690CB00022B/5150